VERMONT
GOLF
COURSES
A Player's Guide

VERMONT
GOLF
COURSES
A Player's Guide

Bob Labbance & David Cornwell

The New England Press
Shelburne, Vermont

Design by Andrea Gray
Maps by Northern Cartographic, Inc.
Photos by Bob Labbance and David Cornwell

ISBN 0-933050-47-X
Library of Congress Catalog Card Number: 87-61132
Printed in the United States of America
Second printing, March 1989

For additional copies of this book or for a catalog
of our New England titles, please write:

The New England Press
P.O. Box 575
Shelburne, Vermont 05482

Contents

INTRODUCTION

Our exploration of Vermont's golf courses began in 1980. In six seasons we traveled 7,590 miles and played each of the courses listed in this book at least twice. As you'd expect, our journey took us through the spectacular mountain passes and beautifully groomed valleys that one can only find in Vermont. But rather than looking for beauty we were looking for golf, and in gathering information a casual pastime quickly turned into an obsession. In fact, if someone lit a course for night play, we'd be first in line—but before long there'd be a wait at the first tee, because golf is becoming ever more popular in Vermont.

There are unique features to golf in a state that is 90 percent forested and that has very few flat acres, features you don't run into in a lifetime of golf in Florida or even Connecticut—like the first three holes at Killington with a combined vertical drop of 315 feet! Or a narrow, steep shoot-up to a green nestled in the woods, like number 13 at Rocky Ridge. Other features—not related to topography—are less unusual. For instance, you'll find few courses in the state that are fully irrigated. That is seldom a problem in a state with abundant rainfall, but brownouts do occasionally occur. Most courses contain a mixture of grasses and thus few have fairways that are a tee-to-green carpet. Further, what constitutes a sand trap is rather loosely interpreted by greenskeepers. Few courses have deep, loose beach sand; fine gravel may be closer to reality in many places.

We've tried to note these (and other) variables in each course entry, but we don't wish to discourage play anywhere. Instead, we concentrate on the ambience, challenge, and outstanding design features of each. And although we've given more coverage to the eighteen-hole facilities, we do not mean to slight the nine-hole clubs. While few of their cards provided a detailed course map that we could use, there's some excellent golf out there, and all provide a great place to learn the game while serving the social needs of many small towns.

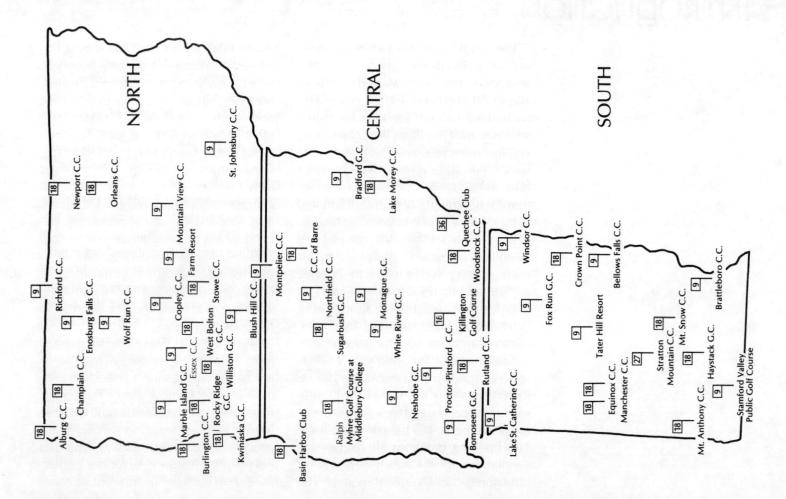

NORTH

CENTRAL

SOUTH

St. Johnsbury C.C.

Newport C.C.

Orleans C.C.

Bradford G.C.

Lake Morey C.C.

Mountain View C.C.

Quechee Club

Windsor

Crown Point C.C.

Richford C.C.

Farm Resort

Bellows Falls C.C.

Enosburg Falls C.C.

Copley C.C.

Stowe C.C.

Montpelier C.C.

C.C. of Barre

Woodstock C.C.

Wolf Run C.C.

Fox Run G.C.

Brattleboro C.C.

Blush Hill C.C.

Northfield C.C.

Tater Hill Resort

Champlain C.C.

West Bolton G.C.

Montague G.C.

Killington Golf Course

Sugarbush G.C.

White River G.C.

Mt. Snow C.C.

Essex C.C.

Williston G.C.

Stratton Mountain C.C.

Marble Island G.C.

Proctor-Pittsford C.C.

Equinox C.C.

Haystack G.C.

Rocky Ridge G.C.

Neshobe G.C.

Alburg C.C.

Manchester C.C.

Burlington C.C.

Rutland C.C.

Kwiniaska G.C.

Ralph Myhre Golf Course at Middlebury College

Basin Harbor Club

Bomoseen G.C.

Lake St. Catherine C.C.

Mt. Anthony C.C.

Stamford Valley Public Golf Course

The book is organized as follows: We've divided the state into three sections—north, central, and south—to allow you to quickly find the course you wish to read about. The map on page 8 tells you which section the course is in, and the index tells you exactly where to look if you have a particular course or town in mind. The map is also useful for those who are in a certain location and want to know which courses are nearby. Within each section, the courses are listed alphabetically. In the listing for each course, we've tried to provide everything you need to know—number of holes, yardages, opening and closing dates, slope, fees, amenities, telephone number, and directions for getting there.

The yardages for nine-hole courses represent two trips around the layout; many clubs vary the same nine by providing a second set of tees, which sometimes even changes the par of the hole. The opening dates for all courses are *very* approximate—much depends on our unpredictable Vermont weather. The prices listed are for the 1988 season and subject to change. You can, however, beat the high cost of an individual round. Memberships are available everywhere and range in price from $100 to $600 for a season's worth of golf. The Vermont Lung Association Golf Privilege Card allows you to play twenty of the forty-three courses on their list free of charge simply by making a $40 donation. Restrictions such as mandatory cart or weekday play only may apply. Call 800–642–3288 for details. The Dividend Card offered by Vermont Dividends, Inc. (802–334–5077), is another way to play an assortment of courses at a discount.

There's also a course map for each of the eighteen-hole courses. These maps are based on the club's scorecard and, as all golfers know, some scorecard maps are more detailed than others. Following each information section is our analysis of the course—its highlights and outstanding features; factors to be prepared for, such as the amount of water or wind; and a look at the toughest holes on the course and how they might be played. In general, we try to give you an idea of the feel of the course. In the back of the book you'll find a history of golf in Vermont (Appendix A), the latest course rating/slope figures for Vermont Golf Association clubs (Appendix B), golf-related activities in Vermont and a survey of courses near Vermont (Appendix C), and the architects of Vermont's golf courses (Appendix D).

Although you'll never find a two-hour wait to tee off, courses can be crowded on weekends. Also, most of the clubs have a weekly league time when it's tough to get out on the course. A few courses limit play to members only at times, foursomes only on weekends, and some close to the public altogether during the club championship. Even if starting times are not required, it's always a good idea to call ahead before you drive a hundred miles only to be disappointed. We've learned this from experience.

While nearly all the clubs sell at least beer and wine, the Vermont Liquor Law states that "there is to be no consumption of alcoholic liquor in any open area, on or in connection with licensed premises, without first obtaining permission from the Liquor Control Board." Therefore the rules allowing you to buy a beer at the clubhouse to take out on the course vary; please ask.

Finally, we'd like to hear from you if you have any suggestions for us as we prepare future editions of this book. Please write us with your comments in care of the publisher. In the meantime, happy golfing!

We haven't duffed our way through Vermont's golf courses without our share of trouble. We've hit maintenance equipment, clubhouses, duck hooks, screaming slices, dribbles that go ten yards, the ground, and double figures on simple, straightforward holes. We've examined the deep rough from Richford to Stamford. And we've lost golf balls everywhere we tell you it's possible, and more. But we've learned it doesn't take great golfing ability to recognize a great golf course. Even so, we couldn't have finished this book without help from the clubs that responded to our survey and questions, and we thank them. We hope we have represented each club fairly. We also couldn't have done it without Stephanie Wolff's darkroom, and we thank her. Special thanks go out to Jim Stone, Jon Kostka, and the Kefferville Country Club, official home of the V.D.A. Dr. Ed Simpson, John Larkin, and Jim Bassett of the Vermont Golf Association provided information. Assistance with writing came from Bill Van Liew and Thomas Powers. Help with historical research has come from Owen V. Baker of Brattleboro Country Club, Janet Seagle at the USGA Golf House Library, Nanette A. Kenrick of the Ouimet Golf Library, Ray Delaney and Floyd James of Burlington, Sally Waters Fisher, Jim Promo, and the library staffs at Morrisville, Rutland, and UVM Special Collections. And the entire project would have been impossible without the understanding of those non-golfers who saw chores go undone while we trouped out for yet another seven-hour excursion.

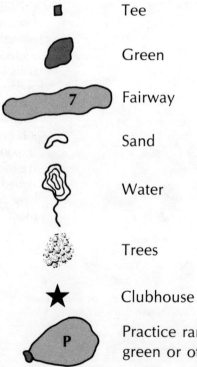

Tee

Green

Fairway

Sand

Water

Trees

Clubhouse

Practice range,
green or other area

**All prices listed are for the 1988
season and subject to change.**

ALBURG C.C.

Established: 1963

Number of Holes: 18

Yardages: Middle, 6287; Forward, 5747

Par: 72, 75

Slope: 109, 97

Fees: $10.00 weekdays ($5.00 after 4:00 P.M.), $12.00 weekends ($6.00 after 3:00 P.M.)

Approximate Season: May 1 to October 31

150-yard markers: Red posts

Carts: Motorized and pull

Starting Times: Not necessary

Amenities: Full food and bar service

Telephone: 796–3586

Directions: On Lake Champlain about 5 miles south of Alburg. From S. Alburg, go about 2.5 miles west on Route 129. Course is on right before crossing bridge to Isle La Motte.

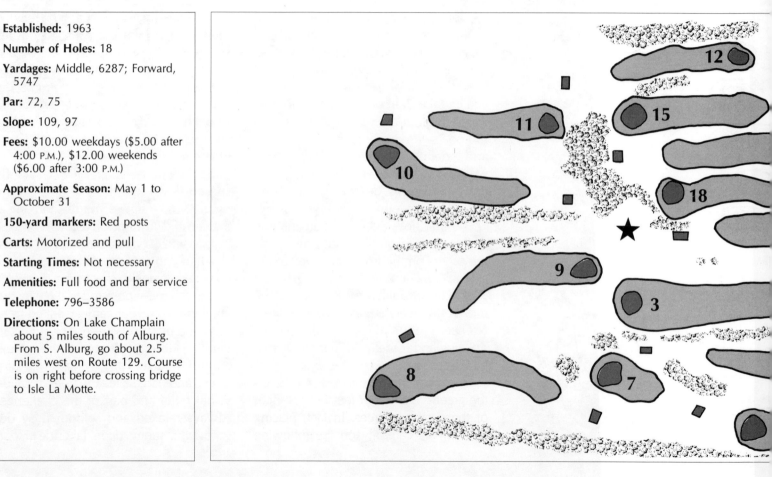

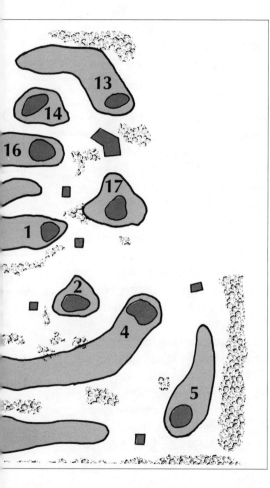

Alburg is a country course situated next to Lake Champlain and subject to the wind and weather found on such a large body of water. Though many holes are flat or gently rolling there is some real terrain on the back nine. You might think that with no out of bounds, not one sand trap or real water hazard, and generally wide-open fairways it would be a pushover. But watch out for the murderously deep rough and four par 4s each well over 400 yards.

The first hole (524 yd. par 5) is one of three par 5s on the front side. It and the others on the front play over gently rolling to flat terrain. Numbers 5, 6, and 7 play up through and down around a more hilly, isolated, and wooded area. Number 11 (295 yd. par 4) begins the undulating and sometimes sharply pitched part of the course. At the long twelfth (447 yd. par 4) you may ask, "Where's the green?" Aim your tee shot just right of those fairway trees. In fact, placing your drives carefully on the following holes is the only way to par. The lengthy fourteenth (179 yd. par 3) starts out flat but quickly moves up onto a crowned and rolling fairway. Stay away from the left side—the rough is too painful. The eighteenth (419 yd. par 4) is a great finishing hole and a real standout. You can see most of the trouble, so you'll know where to place your drive. Almost anything except for a great shot will be sucked down into the low area on the right. Avoid it unless you like looking at a steep hill in front of you as you prepare to hit 200 yards to a perched green.

When you come to Alburg you might consider playing the back nine twice; it's that much more pleasing to the eye and challenging to your game. Created from farmland by the owner-operator Ellison family, Alburg epitomizes the casual country course. Fairways feel like pastures, and large elegant trees provide visual relief and part of the challenge. Always relaxed and seldom busy describes this sunny, open, lakeside layout.

BLUSH HILL C.C. Waterbury

Established: 1919

Number of Holes: 9

Yardages: Middle, 4730; Forward, 4534

Par: 66

Slope: 100, 96

Fees: $9.00 for 9 holes weekdays, $10.00 weekends; $16.00 for 18 holes weekdays, $18.00 weekends

Approximate Season: May 15 to October

150-yard markers: None

Carts: Motorized and pull

Starting Times: Not necessary

Amenities: Full food and bar service

Telephone: 244–8974

Directions: Take Exit 10 from I-89 to Route 100 north; take the first left (Blush Hill Road). Go one mile and the course is on your left with driveway beyond.

The views from Blush Hill are as scenic as any in the state because of its exposure to the nearby Worcester Mountains throughout the layout. A variety of challenging terrains makes it tougher to score than you would think on a course of 4834 yards. There are few gifts among the six par 4s and three par 3s.

The two most difficult holes open the course. Number 1 (378 yd. par 4) heads sharply downhill from the clubhouse, with large rocks jutting out of the ground in many places along the fairway. A raised green with a front lip tilts toward you across a dirt roadway. The second hole (352 yd. par 4) is steadily back uphill. The wide-open tee shot will allow for a variety of views into the small, narrow green. Any second shot will be complicated by an uphill lie and the steep-faced plateau on which the green is perched. The third hole has a feature that is unique to golf in Vermont: a three-hundred-foot radio tower (one of three in a row) that dominates the left side of the fairway. Course rule number 4 states that a "drive from the third tee hitting wires, tower, white fence or white house on fly may be reteed without penalty," but the "psych value" makes for a tougher-than-average 210-yard par 4. The next hole, a downhill 188-yard par 3 with a deep swale in front of a forward-sloping green, is of deceptive distance. Better walk out and take a look at number 6, a blind, downhill, 139-yard par 3. The green can't be seen from the tee and you'll have to carry a row of trees to get there.

Blush Hill dishes out its complications without length or a single sand trap or water hazard. Originally designed by Andrew Freeland as part of the Waterbury Inn, the course has experienced many changes over the years. The low-key casual atmosphere is perfect for a family outing, or the kids can go tour the Ben & Jerry's ice cream factory right down the road while you play. We've had some fine late fall golf there with the greens still in excellent condition. Only two minutes off I–89 and less than two hours to play, Blush Hill is well worth a quick visit.

BURLINGTON C.C.

Established: 1924

Number of Holes: 18

Yardages: Back, 6514; Middle, 6356; Forward, 5699

Par: 71, 73

Slope: 124, 123, 116

Fees: $30.00 plus mandatory cart until 2:00 P.M. Course only open to the public prior to Memorial Day and after Labor Day on weekdays and weekends after 2:00 P.M. (at the discretion of the pro).

Approximate Season: May 1 to mid–October

150-yard markers: Small shrubs on right

Carts: Motorized and pull

Starting times: Recommended at all times

Amenities: Full food and bar service

Telephone: 864–9532

Directions: From UVM main campus, go south on South Prospect St. past Redstone campus approximately one-half mile. Entrance is on left.

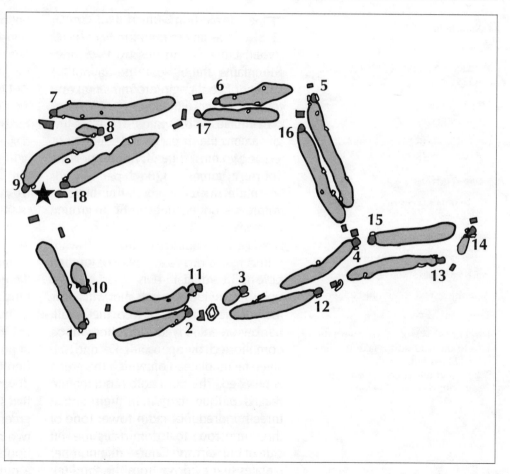

This outstanding Donald Ross course is unique in Vermont for its unusual layout. Links-like in design, two nine-hole loops parallel and cross each other twice in their circle around a private estate. As a result, seldom is any more than the one adjoining hole visible, and there is no claustrophobic bunching of tees and greens. Since BCC is also among the most carefully groomed and very best maintained courses in the state, it's no great wonder that drastic measures were taken in 1985 to limit the traffic and keep the quality of play high.

Burlington boasts a variety of terrains ranging from flat to gently rolling that contain numerous small hidden water hazards. Burlington also remodeled some bunkers in 1986 and 1987 that added even more challenge to its lengthy yardage. The moderate to large-sized greens are well guarded by hazards and, though angled toward fairways, their subtle undulations and dangerous speed add to their reputation for being difficult. The caddie booklet and card available at the clubhouse provide the most comprehensive hole-by-hole overview anywhere in the state and should be worth a few strokes saved if carefully followed.

The opening hole (383 yd. par 4) does not require a long tee shot but it should be straight. The terrain on this hole and number 10, which shares the same rolling gorge, is the most up and down you'll find here, but don't be misled by the lack of hills. Proper placement of your shot is the most important factor in scoring well, and many times you'll find that the apparently wide-open, flat fairways offer only small, preferred landing zones for optimal approach shots. Number 4, a 398-yard par 4, is a good example; seemingly straightforward, it contains hidden trouble off the tee. Just where you'd like to place a nice drive there's a small pond on the left and a mound on the right. This forces all but the longest hitters to play safe and short, leaving 200 yards plus to the small green.

While not the longest par 3 in the state, 197-yard number 10 is one of the toughest. It's all visible from the tee: a narrow tree-lined alley rolling down

The 197-yard tenth hole is one of the toughest par 3s in the state.

most of the way, then back up to a sloping green; traps left, right, and center-front, deep rough and trees behind. The eleventh (333 yd. par 4) has been tightened up considerably with a new large trap carefully placed in fairway center and left to snag anyone trying to cut the corner. Your approach must then carry

a small brook that crosses the fairway twenty yards in front of the green. Number 12 (440 yd. par 4) is one of the longest par 4s in the state. Bunkers guard the left side and you'll need a long high second shot to hold the distant small target. The closing hole (500 yd. par 5) brings you back in style. Traps again frame the driving zone and the approach to the large, sloping green. The uphill sweep makes it tough to get close in two.

One of the top courses in Vermont, Burlington plans to continue its semi-private status. The pro shop reports that restrictions on public access have yielded the sought-after results. While we applaud all efforts aimed at improving the quality of play, costs in excess of $75 for two with cart make BCC out of range for many. Several other clubs in the area offer very enjoyable golf at much more reasonable rates. But with top-flight grooming, slick, smooth putting surfaces, and fairways on which the ball sits up time and time again, Burlington Country Club is well worth a play to the golf connoisseur.

CHAMPLAIN C.C.

Established: 1915

Number of Holes: 18

Yardages: Back, 6145; Middle, 5976; Forward, 5217

Par: 70

Slope: 120, 119, 112

Fees: $15.00 any day, $9.00 after 5:30 P.M. (closed to the public before 11:00 A.M. weekends)

Approximate Season: April 15 to October 30

150-yard markers: Evergreen bushes with an orange tag

Carts: Motorized and pull

Starting Times: Not available

Amenities: Full food and bar service

Telephone: 527–1187

Directions: On the east side of Route 7 four miles north of St. Albans.

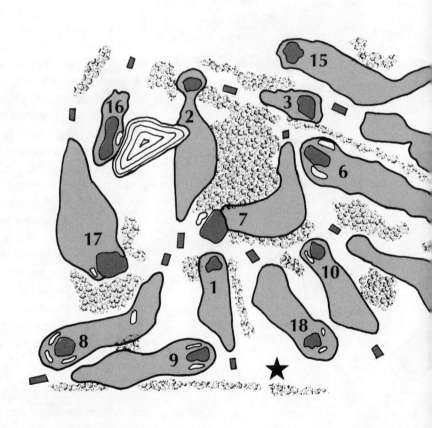

20

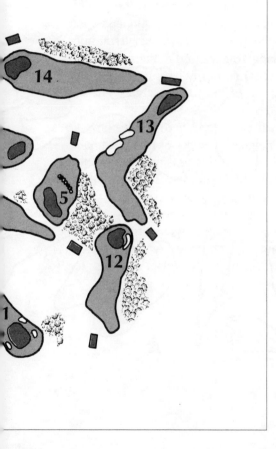

Champlain Golf Club was organized in 1915 and played on nine holes for seventy years until its expansion to eighteen in 1985. Rather than add on an entirely different back nine, Champlain hired Montreal architect Graham Cooke to add nine holes and integrate the whole eighteen into a totally new layout. Therefore the front nine contains five of the old holes, the back nine, four. The fairways of the new holes are tighter than the old but the greens are bigger, and the entire course has taken on a new feel.

What is now the first hole (303 yd. par 4) used to be the par-4 eighth and, with a different set of markers, the par-3 seventeenth. As you'd expect with a former par 3, the hole is narrow and plays to a small green. A row of trees on the right closes in to a large elm that guards the green. The second hole (424 yd. par 4) starts a string of four new holes. A platform is provided so you can climb up to see where the blind tee shot should be aimed. The take-off is narrow but the fairway widens out until it is eventually con-

stricted again by a pond on the left. A full second shot is needed to climb up to the elevated green, which is protected by trees, rough, and a rock outcropping left. The driving area on the 373-yard, par-4 fourth is narrowed by water right and a tree left. The green is fronted by a large mound on the right. On number 6 twin mounds (one cut smooth, the other rough and shaggy when we were there) front the green and affect your approach strategy. The long snake-like fairway on this 552-yard par 5 is moguled and also bordered by trees and a stone wall on the right. The eighth (416 yd. par 4) was the standout hole on the original course. The turn in the dogleg is also the highest point of the fairway, forcing a blind second shot if you hit a short drive. A large fairway trap eliminates the shortcut right, and trees encroach long and left. The large putting surface falls off into traps left, right, and rear.

The back nine features outstanding old and new par 3s. The twelfth (166 yd. par 3), with its narrow exit tee tucked in next

Champlain's new clubhouse opened in June 1988.

bankment. The new 128-yard, par-3 sixteenth is quite a contrast to the twelfth with its wide open fairway and large long green. Here the pond that cut into number 2 is dangerously close to the putting surface, separated only by a trap lodged in the crook of the figure-eight green (see photo).

It will take some time for the new to fully integrate with the old at Champlain, but in time guests will never know the two have been meshed. The new greens with their sand base are not that much quicker than the old humus-based greens. Post-construction tree planting and landscaping are ongoing. As fairway and rough fill in, Champlain readies for another seventy years of golf.

to the woods, is the former third. An elm on the left and a trap on the right frame the very small green that rejects the ball off the back and down a four-foot em-

COPLEY C.C.

Established: 1936

Number of Holes: 9

Yardages: Middle, 5550; Forward, 5020

Par: 70

Slope: 104, 98

Fees: $9.50 weekdays, $11.50 weekends ($5.00 after 5:00 P.M. any day)

Approximate Season: April 15 to October 15

100-yard markers: Blue posts

Carts: Motorized and pull

Starting Times: Not available

Amenities: Full food and bar service

Telephone: 888–3013

Directions: Take Main St. less than one mile east of downtown. Turn right on Maple St. Course entrance 100 yards on left.

Alexander Hamilton Copley was born in Morrisville in 1856. After making his fortune in a pharmacy business and real estate in Boston, he returned to his home town as a wealthy benefactor. In his remaining years he was responsible for revitalizing Peoples Academy, donating funds for Copley Hospital, and creating Copley Country Club. Originally a combination airfield and golf course, the land was crossed by two grass landing strips that remained in occasional use from their opening in 1936 until the Morrisville-Stowe State Airport was completed in 1960. Although this flat plateau slightly above town was perfectly suited for air traffic, conflicts between golfers not clearing fairways quickly enough on the one hand and small plane owners damaging greens and tying planes to the clubhouse on the other eventually spelled an end to joint usage.

Today this broad, flat field still entertains local golf enthusiasts. The layout and numbering of holes has been changed four times in the last fifty years. The two par 3s are both made interesting by unusual greens. Number 2 is a slightly downhill 216-yarder with a large three-level green displayed on an angle towards the tee. The green is surrounded by traps, and a ball lucky enough to run up on the front could easily be putted thrice before it finds a hole cut near the back shelf. The green on number 5 (171 yd. par 3) resembles a 60-foot diameter, perfectly round sheet with a 40-foot square pillow underneath it. Find the wrong part of this one and you'll feel like you're playing miniature golf. The outstanding hole on the layout is the 327-yard, par-4 third. A rippled gorge fifteen to twenty feet deep bisects the fairway on a diagonal. If you hit it long you may clear the gorge on the left side. In any event caution is necessary on your approach to the medium-sized green, which usually rejects the ball off the right rear corner and down a tree-covered hillside.

Resembling British links-style golf, the seventh (373 yd. par 4) is typical of several Copley holes. Seemingly flat, featureless fairways make the judgement of distance difficult and hides danger from the golfer's eyes. A mini-gorge lies beyond the large maple that protects the left-side shortcut on this slight dogleg. Sand traps well before the green are nearly invisible until you're on top of them, and a flat green rejects a fast-moving ball from any direction.

Copley is a course that most anyone can pleasurably stroll around, enjoying mountain views along with a game of golf. Broad fairways lead the way to medium-sized greens. Turf quality is good throughout, and putts travel a bit on the rapid side of average. Keep an eye out for low-flying planes.

Established: 1963

Number of Holes: 9

Yardages: Back, 5680; Middle, 5568; Forward, 5284

Par: 72, 74

Slope: 114, 113, 109

Fees: $10.00 weekdays ($5.00 after 5:00 P.M.), $14.00 weekends and holidays ($7.00 after 5:00 P.M.)

Approximate Season: May 1 to October 31

150-yard markers: Posts

Carts: Motorized and pull

Starting Times: Not available

Amenities: Full food and bar service

Telephone: 933–8951

Directions: Hidden in a residential neighborhood just north of the business district in Enosburg Falls on Route 105.

Another example of an excellent country course with a laid-back atmosphere, Enosburg features outstanding par 5s and par 3s, with some short yet demanding par 4s. With only a few traps and a small bit of strategically placed water, the course draws on substantial terrain on every hole, including rock outcroppings and a slippery sidehill green or two for both fun and challenge.

The second hole (538 yd. par 5) is a long, gradual uphill with a small pond to the right of the drive landing zone, a rock to the left of the second shot area, and a slanted green facing the fairway. The green on the 181-yard, par-3 third can't be seen from the tee because it's over the crest of a rise and completely surrounded by mounding. A well-placed drive on the 266-yard, par-4 fourth will still result in a sidehill lie. The large rolling green with a trap in front and a drop-off behind is bordered by a creek that runs along the right side of this dogleg. At 238 yards, the fifth is the longest par 3 in the state from the white tees. Uphill with a clump of rocks and sumac guarding the right side of the putting surface, this is the number 1 handicap hole. Number 6 (552 yd. par 5) crosses a broad gully on the way to a steeply tilted, sidehill green. You'll need a couple of good shots and a precise putt to steal a par here. And a final word of advice: if you hit it long, don't hit it all at number 8 (282 yd. par 4). The chasm that's hidden from view in front of the green is deep, the grass long, and the water easy to find.

With a sunny clubhouse bar facing out toward the course, reasonable rates, and a separate chipping and putting area, Enosburg is a fun place for all. The layout allows room to spray it around and is therefore accessible to players of all ability levels. With little irrigation, the fairways can become burnt. But in a good year the fairways are a deep, thick mat of grass and the greens uniform, true, and quick.

ESSEX COUNTRY CLUB Essex

Established: 1988

Number of Holes: 9

Yardages: Back, 6498; Middle, 6350; Forward, 5414

Par: 74

Slope: 121, 121, 111

Fees: $8.00 weekdays, $10.00 weekends ($6.00 after 4:00 P.M. any day)

Approximate Season: April 15 to November 15

Carts: Motorized and pull

Starting Times: Not required

Amenities: Full food and bar service

Telephone: 879–3232

Directions: From Essex Junction Five Corners, take Route 15 north for 2 miles. Turn left on Old Stage Road and follow it for 3 miles. Clubhouse is on left.

The Essex Country Club on Old Stage Road in Essex Center is Vermont's newest golf facility. Nine holes opened in the spring of 1988, with nine more in the works for 1989. The routing will be redirected when all eighteen holes are in play, and the existing holes will be renumbered. Graham Cooke of Montreal designed the course and owner Joe Chastenay is directing the multi-year effort to complete the project.

At 580 yards from the rear tees, the first hole is by far the longest hole on the course, and the pain of its length is exacerbated by the need to lay up with your first shot! A driver from the middle tee by an average player would probably land squarely in the midst of unplayable swamp grasses and muck. Take a shorter wood, an easy swing, and be on your way down a fairway narrowed by the road to the left and trees to the right. A large, oval green with a broad, flat approach lies in wait at the end.

The same swampy creek must be negotiated with your tee shot on the 440-yard, par-5 dogleg fifth. If you carry 185 yards off the tee you'll be in position to hit towards the green even though a mound blocks your view. The sixth is the second of the back-to-back par 5s and, at 510 yards, is the one more likely to require three good strokes before you putt. If you don't stay to the right it could be double that.

The par-3 eighth measures a scant 110 yards but 100 of it is carry over water to a large green facing the tee. With sharp embankments left and rear and trees framing a green humped to the right side, there is little room for error here. Bailing out to the right is the only escape.

The greens at Essex are speedy and in excellent shape at such a tender age. Fairways are generous, firm, and well covered with grasses benefiting from full irrigation. There is no sand at present but it will be added when the back nine is completed. With state regulations bringing new course construction to a virtual standstill we heartily congratulate Joe Chastenay for his perseverance in providing a new option to Chittenden County golfers.

THE FARM RESORT

Established: 1969

Number of Holes: 9

Yardages: Back, 6038; Middle, 5798; Forward, 5198

Par: 72

Slope: 111, 108, 106

Fees: $11.00 weekdays, $13.00 weekends ($6.00 after 4:00 P.M. any day)

Approximate Season: April 15 to October 31

150-yard markers: Trees or posts

Carts: Motorized and pull

Starting Times: Available

Amenities: Full food and bar service

Telephone: 888–3525

Directions: On the west side of Route 100 six miles north of Stowe or three miles south of Morrisville.

Only a short drive from the Stowe area, the Farm Resort bridges the gap between the laid-back country course and a sophisticated country club. Here the atmosphere is casual but the golf is top-flight. Originally designed by Geoffrey Cornish in 1969 as an eighteen-hole, par-3 layout, the course fell into disrepair and eventually closed in the early 1980s. Now it has returned as a 3003-yard, par-36 nine-holer with three ponds, ample up and down terrain, and large, deeply sculpted traps on every hole.

The first hole (371 yd. par 4) combines all these elements and forces you to deal with them immediately. A rolling fairway bends around to the right and up a small shelf to a medium-sized green framed by deep-sided traps on the right and a large pond on the left. A mis-hit approach or even a bashed putt could roll clear off this green and into the pond. At 473 yards, the third is a par 5 nearly 100 yards shorter than the sixth, but it's just as tough. The narrow side-hill fairway tilts into deep woods bordering the entire left-hand side. The last hundred yards climbs up to a large, slick, three-level green with another mounded trap to the left. Miss your par on the 151-yard, par-3 fourth and you'll have another chance. The fifth is very similar and seven yards shorter. Both feature elevated tees and narrow putting surfaces guarded by undulating bunkers and mounds directly adjoining the greens.

A tough enough test from the white, Farm Resort also features championship tees that add another couple of hundred yards of rolling terrain and water to carry over. With sixteen large traps, water affecting four holes, frequent mounding and occasional deep woods, this course is no picnic. But the hazards are all in view and the medium-fast greens putt smooth and true. In short, a fair test of the game. With continued care similar to that which has brought it back from the edge of extinction, Farm Resort will grow into one of the premier nine-hole layouts in Vermont over the next few years. Be sure to include it in your next Stowe vacation.

Established: 1965

Number of Holes: 18

Yardages: Back, 7067; Middle, 6796; Forward, 5911

Par: 72

Slope: 125, 122, 117

Fees: $11.00 weekdays ($7.00 after 5:00 P.M.), $14.00 weekends ($11.00 after 5:00 P.M.)

Approximate Season: April 15 to mid-November

150-yard markers: Crabapple trees on both sides

Carts: Motorized and pull

Starting Times: Not available

Amenities: Full food and bar service

Telephone: 985–3672

Directions: Take Webster Road off Route 7 a bit north of Shelburne Center. Go left onto Spear Street; the clubhouse is at the top of the hill.

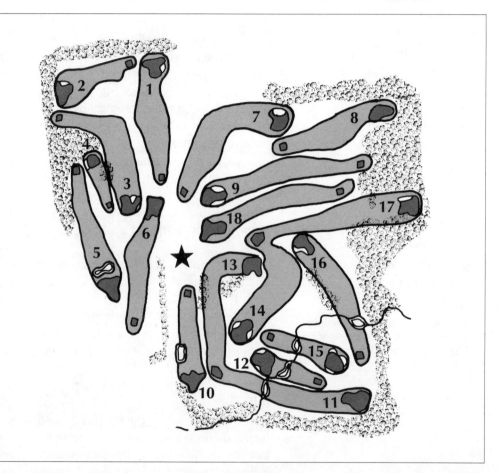

This is one of the longest courses in the state, and also one of the first to open every year. It sits atop a hill within a few miles of Lake Champlain's Shelburne Bay. A large deep gorge affects play on five of the holes on the back side. When you finally find a short par 4 (number 17, 327 yards) there's a tree growing in the middle of the fairway in front of the green. Here we find enough challenge for golfers of all ability levels including the long hitter.

The first six holes sit on the west side of Spear St., the clubhouse and the other twelve holes lie to the east. Number 3 (480 yd. par 5) is the shortest par 5 on the course and invites you to cut the dogleg right corner and get yourself in trouble. Most anyone can hit two good shots on number 5 (465 yd. par 4) and still be in trouble, as a pond sits in front of the green. Without a big drive it's a blind second shot anyway, so be smart and lay up. Even on the PGA Tour this hole would cause some problems. The front nine concludes with an uphill 552-yard, par-5 monster.

The clubhouse has an extensive pro shop, a large bar, and plenty of windows. Since you can see it from much of the course, you can also see many of the holes from it. Better have a beer; the back nine is a bit shorter, but it has many more ups and downs. Number 11 (363 yd. par 4) is a narrow test with water in the fairway and a tough second shot to a green with rough encroaching. The twelfth (181 yd.) and the fifteenth (193 yd.) are both long par 3s that cross the chasm and leave no room for the duffed, topped, or short shot. You finally climb your way out of this potential hell on 16, another par 5 of over 500 yards—which is made even longer by its steady uphill progression.

With its length, five elevated greens, and the ample terrain that provides many sidehill lies, Kwiniaska is a tough layout and a long walk for most average golfers. The sand, which resembles fine

This hidden pond fronts the fifth green on the longest par 4 in the state.

white gravel, does not come into play much, but a stiff breeze blowing off the lake certainly could. The area is wide open, with few trees on the interior of the course and little hole-to-hole isolation. The ball sits up well in the fairway and the greens are of medium speed. No matter how you do, the scenery is nice and it's one of the best 18-hole values in the state. Built, owned, and operated since 1965 by Brad Caldwell, the Kwiniaska Golf Club has absorbed the overflow from the Burlington area. In this capacity and as a proving ground for those long-ball hitters, it will continue to flourish in the years ahead.

MARBLE ISLAND G.C.

Established: c. 1920

Number of Holes: 9

Yardages: Back, 5228; Middle, 5086; Forward, 4436

Par: 66

Slope: 111, 110, 103

Fees: $7.00 for 9 holes, $10.00 for 18 holes weekdays ($6.00 after 5:00 P.M.), $9.00 for 9 holes, $12.00 for 18 holes weekends

Approximate Season: May through October

150-yard markers: White stakes

Carts: Pull

Starting Times: Not necessary

Amenities: Full food and bar service

Telephone: 864–4546

Directions: Take Marble Island Road north off Route 127 in Colchester.

A Malletts Bay resort offering a marina, lodging, tennis, and swimming, Marble Island has an A. Tillinghast-designed nine-hole course as well. Only minutes north of Burlington on Lake Champlain you'll find a short layout of four par 3s and only one par 5. While mostly level there is some hillside along the field-like fairways. A natural setting just off the water means wind can be a big factor. In addition, Marble Island has recently established a new sequence of its 9-hole layout, adding some new tees and hazards.

The fourth hole, a 135-yard par 3, plays from a narrow, secluded teeing ground in the woods down to a green surrounded by sand traps. A straight, precise tee shot is required here. The 425-yard, par-4 fifth just keeps on bending around to the left, and since you must hit straight down the middle of a tree-lined fairway, a wood may be needed to reach this small green in two.

The sixth hole is an upwards 170-yard par 3 to a hidden green fronted on the left first by a pot bunker, then by a steep-sided trap. A large tree stands guard on the right side. Number 7 (300 yd. par 4) moves sharply uphill to an elevated green set into a hillside.

Marble Island Resort offers much more than just 9 holes of golf. Sail on in from New York State or Canada. Entertain the whole family with nearby miniature golf or a swim in the pool or the lake. Take a leisurely hike along the shore. But remember to call ahead during the busy summer season on Lake Champlain.

MOUNTAIN VIEW C.C.　　　　　Greensboro

Established: 1898

Number of Holes: 9

Yardages: Middle, 5538; Forward, 4878

Par: 70

Slope: 110, 105

Fees: $7.00 weekdays, $10.00 weekends for members; $15.00 any day for the public

Approximate Season: June to September

150-yard markers: None

Carts: Motorized and pull

Starting Times: Not necessary

Amenities: Light food and full bar service

Telephone: 533–9294

Directions: Turn from Lake Road left onto Golf Course Road one mile southwest of Greensboro.

In 1898, when Mountain View was organized, it was not at all uncommon to see farm animals grazing on fairways. Such was the case in Greensboro where the farmer who rented the land to the club retained the right to pasture his cows anywhere except on the greens, which were enclosed by barbed wire. What *is* unusual however is that this arrangement continued until 1960 when Mountain View finally purchased the land the course occupied. Although the ambulatory hazards are gone, the club retains its casual and historic atmosphere in this especially beautiful area of Vermont.

Although the holes have been rearranged a couple of times, these golfing grounds have been in continual use for nearly ninety years. The fairway on number 2 (300 yd. par 4) has as many moguls as any ski slope in the state. It gently rises in two steps, and there is literally not a flat spot the entire length except for the green. Large rocks on the left divide the fairway from deep woods. The third is a 146-yard par 3 with the tee perched forty-five feet above a small rolling green. Number 4 (410 yd. par 4) is the first hole in which a long, straight drive is needed. Deep woods border the left of a fairway that rolls down to the right. Then the hole doglegs left where mounds serve to hide and protect the green. Another long drive is called for on the 400-yard, par-4 sixth. Here you shoot blindly over the crest of a hill, with trees and underbrush on the right. The stance for your second shot will invariably be uncomfortable as you hit to a large green tilted towards fairway right. Number 8 (320 yd. par 4) features a Williston Effect tree (see Williston G.C. entry for an explanation of the reference) smack in the middle of the moguled uphill fairway. The plateaued ball-rejecting green fits firmly in the category "tiny." From this unique spot you have a birds-eye view of nearby Caspian Lake and the surrounding mountains.

This is a charming and fun spot for a round of golf. The course presents some challenges, and does so with one small pond and no sand traps. The greens are old-fashioned, small, and of medium speed. The fairways feel like ancient peat bogs in places, and everything is well grown in, including the encroaching woods. Of all the older courses in the state, Mountain View has best preserved that feeling of a bygone era. Bring your plus fours and hickory sticks.

NEWPORT C.C.

Established: 1927

Number of Holes: 18

Yardages: Middle, 6219; Forward, 5544

Par: 72

Slope: 117, 110

Fees: $12.50 weekdays, $15.00 weekends ($7.00 after 5:00 P.M. any day)

Approximate Season: April 15 to October 15

150-yard markers: Red cedar posts

Carts: Motorized and pull

Starting Times: Not available

Amenities: Full food and bar service

Telephone: 334–2391

Directions: From Exit 27 on I-91, head toward Newport on the access road. About ½ mile from the highway turn left onto Clyde Road. Go 2/10 mile and take a right onto Mt. Vernon Street. Course is ½ mile away on left. From downtown, go about ½ mile out Mt. Vernon. The course is on the right.

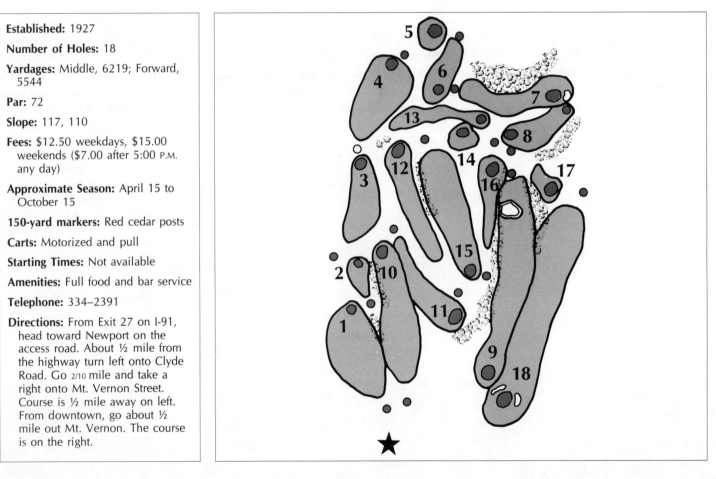

Located on a hilltop overlooking Newport and Lake Memphremagog, Newport Country Club is the state's most northerly eighteen holes, being only five air miles from Canada. (Richford's nine holes are actually closer to Canada). Most of the fairways are laid out along the flat-to-gently rolling upland plateau, so difficult terrain is a factor on a minority of holes. Fairways are open to wide, especially on the front nine, and there is a good measure of bounce and run due to the windswept, firm ground. Evergreen and some deciduous trees line and enclose the greens, offering some windbreak at ground level as well as trouble for those further afield. With only man-made ponds for water and about twenty traps, the test derives from tricky approaches, precise shots to smooth and quick greens, and the ever-present breeze.

The 401-yard, par-4 seventh is the second longest par 4 and is rated the number 1 handicap hole. The bend of the dogleg left is reachable with a good tee shot, but the approach will still be blind. There's a marker to give direction, but it's best to walk up to see the sharp break downhill all the way to the very small green. Trees trouble the left side, a big trap waits behind, and there's just a little room on the right.

Number 8 at 312 yards is the shortest par 4. A dogleg, it climbs back up alongside the seventh hole. The approach here is blind too because of the elevation, but the green is flat and of medium size. The 476-yard ninth is the first of four par 5s, each under 490 yards. The take-off on this one is narrow and goes over a visible small pond. The fairway widens and then gathers back in, particularly on the right side towards the green. Though it's reachable in two, you won't be able to see the putting surface from your tee shot because the fairway rolls down and then up a tad to the small green.

The front nine takes you around the perimeter of the layout, and the back nine plays over the inside. The fairways

Newport C.C. overlooks beautiful Lake Memphremagog.

here are narrower due to trees and traps. Number 18 (471 yd. par 5) is another hole reachable in two. Your tee shot is aimed left to avoid trees and finishes there because the fairway rolls gently leftward. If you are able to drive down the right side, you can hit a fairway wood down the throat of the medium-sized, trap-flanked green.

Newport's open and exposed links afford beautiful views and an enjoyable, airy round. But if the wind is strong, you'll find it a real challenge. Though tee times are not given, you may want to call ahead to check on play, as the course can be quite busy in season.

ORLEANS C.C.

Established: 1926

Number of Holes: 18

Yardages: Back, 6123; Middle, 5934; Forward, 5545

Par: 72, 73

Slope: 117, 115, 111

Fees: $12.00 weekdays, $14.00 weekends (9 holes after 5:00 P.M. is half price any day)

Approximate Season: May 1 to October 31

150-yard markers: Evergreen bushes

Carts: Motorized and pull

Starting Times: Required

Amenities: Full food and bar service

Telephone: 754–2333

Directions: From Downtown Orleans take Route 58 east for about 1½ miles. Turn right on Hollow Road, which the course straddles in less than a mile.

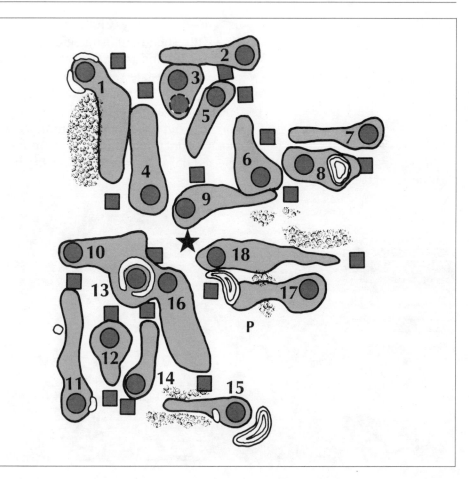

Orleans Country Club proves that with subtle but strategic use of sand, water, and trees, a relatively flat piece of real estate can become a challenging and interesting golf course. There is a small bit of up-and-down terrain here but it's a long way from Vermont mountain golf. Instead there are selected hazards placed to allow for the enjoyment of a round by many, and yet fully reward the play of a precise few. It's such a fair test that Orleans has hosted the Vermont Men's Amateur six times since 1960, including an appearance in 1987. To prepare for that event, management replaced the eighth green and lengthened the fifteenth hole in 1986.

The course opens with a 444-yard par 5. There's about as much interesting terrain on this hole as any at Orleans—an elevated tee, roll-off to the woods left, and a nestled little platform green. If it were to appear later in the layout, after more warm-up, one might be tempted to go for the green in two. Don't. Lay up in front and pitch on or your penalty will be certain sand, or worse. The back nine also opens with an interesting hole. The flat 203-yard, par-3 tenth continually narrows to a green fenced in on the right and back. You can run the ball up between the two flanking traps, but the whole area is actually smaller than it looks from the tee. Number 11 (484 yd.

Construction of the new eighth green.

par 5) epitomizes Orleans. A seemingly flat and straight hole is dotted with enough hazards to make it interesting— first a fairway trap squarely in the driving zone, then hidden, sharply rolling terrain before the green. And the green itself: it's small with evergreens overhanging it on the right, a large trap embracing it left, and out of bounds down an abrupt incline behind. The thirteenth is a unique 140-yard par 3. The only break in a ring of two-foot-tall mounds with accompanying sand traps is a path to walk in onto the green. Lengthened in 1986, the dogleg-right fifteenth hole now plays about 325 yards. However, unlike many of the holes, it is narrow with overhanging tall trees and downhill. Its new medium-sized rolling green is guarded by low mounds left and right, and it is steeply banked down into a pond on the right and rear. A word of caution about retrieving balls from this water hazard: remember that beavers can be very nasty when provoked.

Orleans will render an enjoyable round of golf to players of many ability levels. The fairways as a whole are broad, the rough light between adjoining holes. The walk is easy, the tall trees and scenery pleasant. The fees themselves are a welcome relief, being nearly the lowest in the state. The food is well prepared and there are few better places to enjoy it than on the clubhouse porch overlooking the eighteenth fairway.

RICHFORD C.C. Richford

Established: c. 1930

Number of Holes: 9

Yardages: Middle, 6002; Forward, 5700

Par: 74

Slope: 113, 112

Fees: $10.00 weekdays, $12.00 weekends ($6.00 after 5:00 P.M. any day)

Approximate Season: May 1 to October 31

100-yard markers: Red stakes

Carts: Motorized and pull

Starting Times: Not necessary

Amenities: Full food and bar service

Telephone: 848–3527

Directions: On the Vermont-Quebec border. Go north out of Richford on Route 139 about one mile. Make a right (miss it and you'll be at the border). Go another mile and the clubhouse is on your left.

For those who live in or are traveling through the very north-central part of Vermont, Richford C.C. is a wild and woolly treat. Seldom busy (except at league times), this course features hilly terrain, hole-to-hole separation, and gorgeous mountain views. You know you're near Canada when the score card has local rules in French!

Holes 1 and 2 run back down along the road to town. Seemingly wide open, Richford's deep rough, mounds, undulations, and rock outcroppings lurk in every direction. Play up short on number 2 (464 yd. par 5), as it falls off quickly behind. The 410-yard, par-4 fifth offers a magnetic gorge and trees on the right to grab your tee shot. A long uphill shot to a flat medium-sized green remains.

The seventh (276 yd. par 4) also has a hidden gorge, but at least you have an allowance of two club lengths from the fence your drive will likely roll down to. Stay to the center-right on number nine because cutting the corner puts you in deep rough and you'll need a clean approach shot to hold the green.

Richford's hilliness, mounds, and rocks in the fairway are quintessentially Vermont mountain golf. With a rough-edged quality—yet more than adequately maintained—there's no doubt that this is a fair test. Small, medium-fast greens, natural fairways, and a mixture of grasses and wildflowers all contribute to a casual country atmosphere. And there's no stuffiness around the course or clubhouse, just lots of local color.

ROCKY RIDGE G.C.

St. George

Established: 1961

Number of Holes: 18

Yardages: Middle, 5938; Forward 5236

Par: 72

Slope: 120, 114

Fees: $11.00 weekdays, $12.00 weekends

Approximate Season: April 1 to November 1

150-yard markers: Gray plastic pipes with yellow and blue stripes

Carts: Motorized and pull

Starting Times: Recommended weekends

Amenities: Full food and bar service

Telephone: 482–2191

Directions: On the west side of Route 116, ten miles south of Burlington and three miles north of Hinesburg.

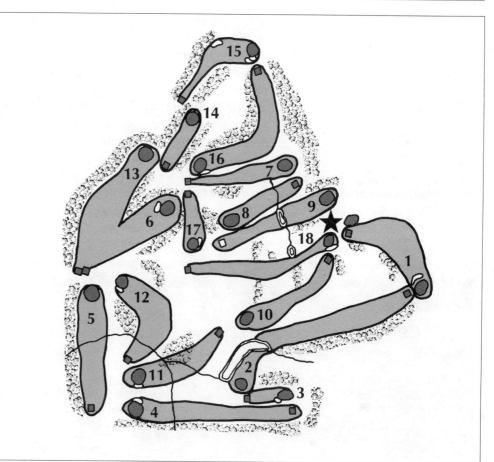

Of all the courses in the Burlington area, Rocky Ridge typifies the diamond in the rough. Not as meticulously groomed as Burlington, or as carefully landscaped as Williston, or as long and rolling as Kwiniaska, Rocky Ridge nonetheless has its own country charm. A moderate number of hazards, rolling to quite hilly terrain, mixed grass fairways, and medium-speed greens all sound a call for thoughtful shotmaking.

View uphill from the tee shared by the sixth and thirteenth holes at Rocky Ridge.

At 270 yards, number 1 might seem an easy par 4 if not for the power lines and poles which cross mid-fairway (even though you may re-tee without penalty if hit). This can leave you with an unpredictable approach to a small, trapped green. The open rolling character of the early holes may lull you into trouble on the 314-yard, par-4 fifth where a hidden creek makes a cut across the fairway. A midiron tee shot is the smart way to play here. Unfortunately tight but interesting is the area around the fifth and twelfth greens and the shared sixth and thirteenth tee (see photograph). Number six (252 yd. par 4) is short but well equipped for trouble. Even a long tee shot yields a sidehill lie as the hole runs steeply uphill to a small perched green. Water frames the landing area for your drive on the 345-yard, par-4 ninth. If you lay up you're left with a long wood to an elevated green tightly bordered by trees and thick rough.

On the back side, the 367-yard, par-4 thirteenth parallels the upsweep of the adjoining sixth and then goes 100 yards further. The small bilevel green above you is closely framed by woods. No need for any sand or water here—it's mountain terrain golf on the number 1 handicap hole. The tee on the 318-yard, par-4 fifteenth is set high above the fairway; dare to cut the corner over the trees to get close to the green. Everything is in view on the 163-yard, par-3 seventeenth from the elevated tee, but choose that iron carefully as there's trouble surrounding the putting surface on all sides. Number 18 (513 yd. par 5) is an excellent long, uphill finishing hole. Proper placement of your second shot is the only way to get a good approach to the hidden and guarded green.

Back in the clubhouse after your round you'll better understand how 5938 yards can play to a real par 72. Designed, built, owned, and operated by Ernest Farrington, the course has become very popular since its 1961 opening. Playability for all levels, reasonable rates, and proximity to the Burlington area all contribute to its reputation. A busy weekday league schedule and a full calendar of weekend events makes it advisable to call ahead anytime during its long seven-month season.

Established: 1923

Number of Holes: 9

Yardages: Middle, 6064; Forward, 5786

Par: 70, 74

Slope: 114, 103

Fees: $12.00 weekdays ($6.00 after 6:00 P.M.), $15.00 weekends

Approximate Season: April 20 until the snow flies

150-yard markers: Yellow stakes on right

Carts: Motorized and pull

Starting Times: Recommended weekends

Amenities: Full food and bar service

Telephone: 748–9894

Directions: Course is on west side of Route 5, six miles north of St. Johnsbury.

St. Johnsbury illustrates the fact that a nine-hole course can offer just as much as an eighteen-hole facility. There's ample room provided for all types of shots and complete privacy from other holes as well. There's not a flat spot or boring hole on the layout. Beautiful views can be had from several elevated tees, and from two sets of tees the course plays differently and stretches out over 6014 challenging yards. Throw in some top flight maintenance and landscaping and you have a destination well worth the travel time.

A dogleg with a sharper angle than number 1 would double back towards the tee. Since it's also steeply uphill there's little chance of driving the green on this 290-yard, par-4 opening hole. A walk through the woods and you're on the scenic second tee with views to the hills behind Lyndonville. Your drive from here will hopefully find a home on the crowned fairway below. A swale in front and a line of trees on the left protect the green 341 yards away. Hit it straight and long uphill from the blind teeing ground at number 4. The last half of this 429-yard par 4 is downhill to a well-bunkered green. The table-top green on the 179-yard, par-3 seventh is about as steeply banked in front as they get, and you've got to carry all the way to get to it. But one-half club too much and you're in the woods behind. This hole requires a placement shot of a length many of us are not comfortable with. There's a final grand view from the very elevated ninth tee. This 391-yard par 4 leads you around the corner and back to the large old white house that serves as clubhouse.

St. Johnsbury C.C. stands as the sole Vermont design by golfer, club-maker, and architect Willie Park, Jr., of Musselburgh, Scotland. Winner of the British Open in 1887 and 1889, Park designed seventy courses in North America between the end of World War I and his death in 1925, including the famous Maidstone G.C. on Long Island, New York. Like all fine layouts, St. Jay is accessible to all but rewarding to the precise few.

STOWE C.C.

Established: 1956

Number of Holes: 18

Yardages: Back, 6156; Middle, 5772; Forward, 5346

Par: 71, 74

Slope: 122, 121, 115

Fees: $30.00 ($20.00 after 3:00 P.M.) any day; $13.00 after 5:00 P.M. 6/15–9/15

Approximate Season: May through October

150-yard markers: Crabapple trees on both sides

Carts: Motorized and pull

Starting Times: Required

Amenities: Full food and bar service

Telephone: 253–4893

Directions: One mile northwest of Stowe Village on Route 108.

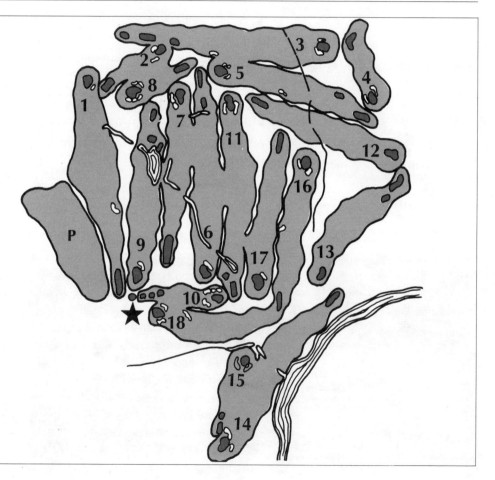

If you're looking for a fine introduction to Vermont mountain golf start at the Stowe Country Club. There may not be quite as much mountainous terrain as a few other courses in the state, but there are only a couple of holes anyone would call flat. With thirty-six sand traps, water on ten holes, out of bounds on eight, and woods surrounding, the course is no easy touch. But fairways have room for errant shots, many greens are accepting and relatively flat, and there's only 5829 yards of course to negotiate from the white tees.

Starting a layout with a par 5 and a par 3 is a good concept to get play going, especially on a resort course. Your first shot on number 1 (482 yd. par 5) is toward a directional flag at the crest of a hill. From there it's downhill for your second and then back uphill to the green. The side-sloping 152-yard, par-3 second plays longer than it looks from the tee. By the time you complete it and gaze out over the rest of the course, you'll have an idea of the kind of terrain facing you here. Originally designed as a par 5, the third hole was built as a very difficult par 4 when Stowe believed it did not own the land that would sustain the first fifty yards of the fairway. The title is now in hand, and in 1989 this hole will finally play as architect William Mitchell planned it over thirty years ago. Out of bounds still runs the length of the

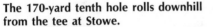
The 170-yard tenth hole rolls downhill from the tee at Stowe.

left side and the small creek which crosses the fairway in its last fifty yards will still snag many shorter shots.

There are holes to make par on between number 3 and number 9 (370 yd. par 4), where after driving over a pond your second shot is toward the clubhouse—if only you could see it. There's another blind second shot on number 12 (371 yd. par 4) but this time the putting surface is below you. You'll have to walk all the way to the edge of the hill to see the top of the flagstick. The fairway on number 13 (327 yd. par 4) is bowl-like, bending towards the flat, figure-eight green. For the sixteenth (352 yd. par 4), picture three mounds with valleys between. The first mound is the tee, the second your landing area, the third the green. Add a few bunkers in front and trees behind and you have the number 2 handicap hole.

The private country club feel is much in evidence here. The pro shop is extensive, the facilities clean and ample, the bar and food service professional. The course is maintained beautifully by a fleet of new equipment. The golf is challenging yet fair, the greens smooth and of medium speed. It's a vigorous walk for anyone not accustomed to mountain golf. There's a driving range and practice area, and diversions for the non-golfer in the Stowe area are many.

WEST BOLTON G.C.

Established: 1983

Number of Holes: 18

Yardages: Middle, 5432; Forward, 5074

Par: 70, 71

Slope: 109, 103

Fees: $7.50 weekdays, $9.00 weekends

Approximate Season: May 1 to November 1

Carts: Motorized and pull

Starting Times: Not available

Amenities: Limited food and beverage service

Telephone: 434–4321

Directions: From Route 2, turn onto Bolton Notch Road 1½ miles west of Bolton. Go 5 miles north through the woods. Course is on left.

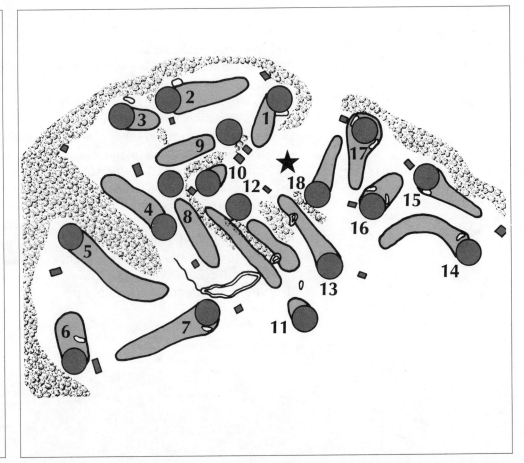

Originally called Mountain View (and with good reason) when opened as a nine-hole course in 1983, the renamed West Bolton G.C. completed its back nine in 1985. The front has grown in well, and even the newer nine was remarkably playable soon after its introduction. Though for the most part gently rolling, there are quite hilly and also flat areas. Besides water and sand, rocky outcroppings appear along fairways and green-side to add further challenge to the rather short layout.

If you have any doubts about 481 yards playing as a strong par 5, the second hole's tiny raised green should put them to rest. The 248-yard, par-4 fourth's elevated and secluded tee gives full view of the long expanse of sidehill lies, some quite steep, that you must carry to achieve a short and level approach to the raised green with its sharply sloped back. Hole number 5 (376 yd. par 4) doglegs right, and only the longest corner-cutting drive will give you even a hint of where they've hidden the green. You might walk ahead to see down the slope into the pocket on the right that contains the green. Number 10, a short 128-yard par 3, starts out along a rock-studded fairway to a U-shaped green that is unique in Vermont. Cradled in the interior is a pint-sized area of rocks and rough, and a bold shot could come to rest there. Number 11 at 430 yards is another short par 5 that still yields a good test. With an elevated tee leading onto a tree-lined fairway, the hole contains a hidden pond on the left just over the rise. More rock outcroppings are directly in play along the way up to and around the green. Number 14 (372 yd. Par 4) begins the flat section of the back nine with a wide and full bend around a working farm. A cottage-sized boulder squarely in center fairway (see photograph) complicates your approach to this small, sloping, and trapped green.

With greens fees at nine-hole courses heading well beyond single digits, it's

Large rocks figure prominently in West Bolton's design.

worth the drive out to inexpensive West Bolton. A short course of moderate terrain with a gorgeous view of the Mount Mansfield Range, West Bolton is the most secluded course in the state. Pro Marty Keene has a very active instructional program, including a Golf Day Camp for youths aged eight to sixteen during June and July.

Established: 1927

Number of Holes: 18

Yardages: Back, 5504; Middle, 5206; Forward, 4738

Par: 69, 72

Slope: 118, 113, 106

Fees: $11.00 weekdays, $13.00 weekends

Approximate Season: May 1 to mid-November

150-yard markers: White posts
100-yard markers: Red posts

Carts: Motorized and pull

Starting Times: Required weekends

Amenities: Full food and bar service

Telephone: 878–3747

Directions: One-half mile off Route 2 on N. Williston Road.

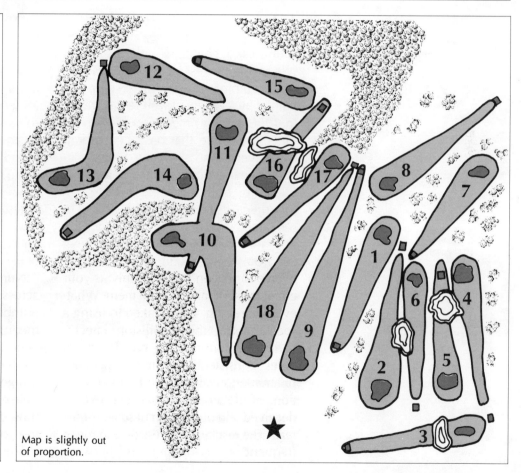

Map is slightly out of proportion.

How do they do it? The landscaping and grooming of the Williston Golf Club could compete with the much pricier resort courses. Lush fairways (due to an automatic watering system) are framed by a variety of well-tended trees. In 1960 a front nine was added to an older back nine that has been rebuilt extensively. And the short hitters can relax—neither of the two par 5s are over 500 yards from the deepest tee.

Perhaps it's because the holes tend to run on the shorter side, or maybe it's the trees that look twenty-five to thirty feet tall from the tee and then shrink to twelve to sixteen feet suddenly as your errant tee shot sails through them. Whatever the reason, we've taken to using a special term, the "Williston Effect," named in honor of the course whose holes consistently exhibit a peculiar phenomenon: an apparent miniaturization of detail such that the eye is deceived and proportion of scale is misread. The resulting impression can mean frequent overclubbing as fairways narrow, close, and bend somehow much more quickly *after* the ball has taken flight.

Many of the front nine's fairways are lined with lovely older willows and long-needled pines. Very playable light rough (and open land under most trees) means that mis-hit tee shots can be easily found and hit out. Number 6 (190 yd. par 3) has a ten-by-twenty-yard pond hidden on the high side of the fairway and further on towards the green a lone tree bounds that same left side. A trap guards front-right, and a mound the back of the left-to-right-sloping putting surface.

Number 11, a 180-yard par 3, plays across a rolling trough, which is actually number 10's approach fairway, up to a medium-sized green that rolls off into large flanking left and right traps. The left-hand trap, while not deep, features a large fir tree squarely in its middle. This hole epitomizes the Williston Effect: just how tall did you think those trees behind the green were?

The 265-yard, par-4 thirteenth is not

An illustration of the Williston Effect on the sixteenth hole.

small green is restricted to a chute about five yards wide closely guarded by two long, undulating traps.

Take a long look at the picture-perfect sixteenth (110 yd. par 3)—the fourth par 3 on the back nine—and remember the Williston Effect as you choose your iron. (See photograph.) If you feel a little discouraged by 380-yard, par-4 number 17's water, walk back to where the championship tee would be. Perhaps this will relax you for the 120 yard-plus carry from the white tee. The water follows the rolling fairway's left side up to the green, an open plateau encircled by evergreens.

When you return to Williston for another visit, you'll probably be struck anew by the lush fairways, attractive landscaping, and deceptive distances. Yet the par-69 5206 yards is very playable for all levels. Williston's unique charm exerts its influence over many area golfers, so call ahead in season—especially on weekends.

the easy hole the numbers might suggest. A tight dogleg on such a short hole is further narrowed by a roll-off into woods at the inside turn and a hedgerow of poplars lining the easily reached outside bend. Your approach to this

Established: 1985 (opened 1987)

Number of Holes: 9

Yardages: Middle, 5940; Forward, 5220

Par: 70, 72

Slope: 115

Fees: $12.00 weekdays, $14.00 weekends ($7.00 after 4:00 P.M. any day)

Approximate Season: May to October

150-yard markers: Brown and white stakes

Carts: Motorized and pull

Starting Times: May be necessary

Amenities: Full food and bar service

Telephone: 933–4007

Directions: On Old Boston Post Road one mile north of Bakersfield.

Wolf Run, one of the newest courses in Vermont, has grown in quickly since its opening in May 1987, and there are nine more holes to come. In addition to the golfing facilities, designer/owner Pete Bandel has now installed cross-country and downhill skiing trails.

The golf course is set upon rolling terrain with postcard views of the surrounding mountains. Certain of its features call to mind the links of yesteryear. The contours are entirely natural, with little evidence of heavy equipment. The tees are set for the most part on small, low mounds. Old stone walls and mature trees border perimeter fairways. Gently sloped small greens sit atop low plateaus with squared off corners. There's an open, park-like feel, though tree plantings will soon provide some hole-to-hole definition.

The first hole, a short par 4 of 315 yards, is one of the tighter tests. The tee shot doesn't need to be long but it ought to be to the left. A dogleg right then leads through a narrow, tree-lined approach to a small green that runs lengthwise away from you. Take advantage of the hazardless green and short distance here, because the next hole is a par 4 of 445 yards! The fifth hole is only a little longer at 460 yards, but here it is a par 5. There is a small creek and pond 180 yards off the tee; carry this and you still must avoid a fairway trap to the right of the landing zone. Up ahead you'll find what we believe is the smallest green of any par 5 in the state; it's guarded by two traps on the right. Though greenside dangers are few, the greens remain tough targets because of their small size and fast speeds.

As work progresses on the next nine holes, scheduled to open in 1990, more traps will be added to those now in play. Pete Bandel was assisted by Gary Bond (the former pro at Stowe) and James Beckett, both graduates of the PGA's golf architectural school, in the design of the first nine holes. Designed by Canadian architect John Watson, the new nine holes at Wolf Run will be his first work in this country outside of Florida.

CENTRAL

BASIN HARBOR CLUB

Established: 1927

Number of Holes: 18

Yardages: Back, 6513; Middle, 6232; Forward, 5805

Par: 72

Slope: 122, 120, 116

Fees: $20.00 weekdays, $22.00 weekends ($10.00 after 4:30 P.M. any day)

Approximate Season: June 1 to mid-October

150-yard markers: Wood stakes

Carts: Motorized and pull

Starting Times: Required

Amenities: Full food and bar service

Telephone: 475–2311

Directions: From Route 22A just south of downtown Vergennes, take a right on Panton Road and another right onto Basin Harbor Road. Course is about five miles ahead.

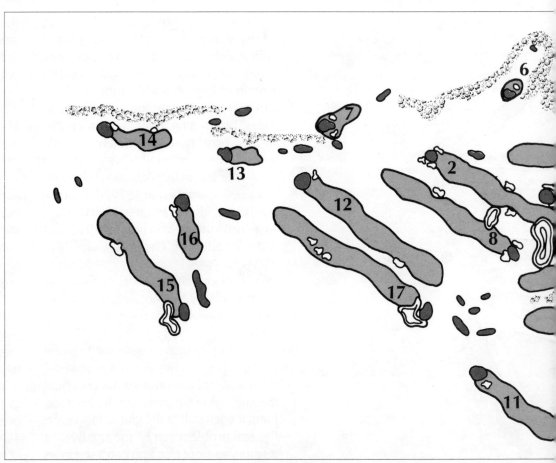

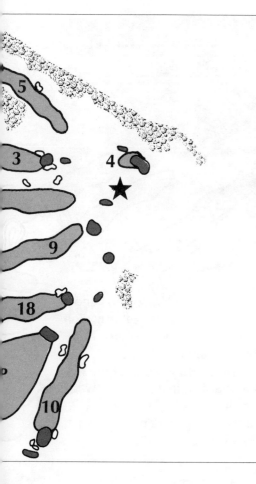

The Basin Harbor Club of Vergennes has occupied seven hundred acres of prime Lake Champlain frontage since 1909. This family-run resort operates from mid-June to mid-October and features a main lodge and sixty-five cottages, swimming pool, tennis courts, beach, boating, and an eighteen-hole golf course. Originally designed as a nine-hole layout by Scotsman Alexander "Nipper" Campbell in 1927, the course has been added to and remodeled twice, first by William Mitchell in 1952 and most recently by Geoffrey Cornish in 1981. This may be the only course in the state you can drive, boat, or fly to, as there is also a 3200-foot air strip for those with a plane and a need for a quick round.

How can a straight, nearly flat 103-yard par 3 with a huge green be trouble? Well, number 6 is simply a narrow chute through some tall trees which also overhang the left half of the green. However, the real problem can be the small bit of territory in front that you can't see from the tee. Crossing the fairway is a greenside sand trap facing an inlaid rock face that could bounce a slightly short hit any which way. In contrast to this sixty-year-old hole is the new seventh, a 150-yard par 3 opened for play in 1986. Here a completely mounded fairway is wide open, and five massive traps engulf the green. The only trees in play are a stand of pines behind the large putting surface. Advice for number 9 (475 yd. par 5): stay right with your drive to skirt the pond, left with your second for a good look at the green, and avoid the green-side gully with the tree in it at all costs. The teeing ground for number 15 (414 yd. par 4) is the closest Vermont golf gets to Lake Champlain. Your drive back inland must clear 100 yards of marshy waste area and contend with a trap wrapped around a mound in the prime landing zone. It's still a long way to the green, which is embraced by a pond ten feet off to the right. This 40-yard-long border starts well in front of the green and entices any nearby golf

The green at the new seventh hole.

ball down to the water. The sixteenth is notable for its 85-yard-long snake-like tee which can create a par 3 anywhere from 140 to 225 yards. Finally, on the seventeenth (510 yd. par 5) you contend with water for the last time. Not merely satisfied to border the hole, an arm protrudes across the entire front of the green, eliminating the option of rolling one on.

The fairways should be settled in now after some remodeling and irrigation work in the mid-1980s. The greens are close-cut and rapid. Without any hilly terrain, Basin Harbor is one of the few courses in the state that is easy to walk. Come on up and stay for a week with the whole family, or for an afternoon of sunny, lakeside golf.

BOMOSEEN G.C.

Established: 1953

Number of Holes: 9

Yardages: Middle, 5010; Forward, 4420

Par: 70

Slope: 107, 101

Fees: $11.00 weekdays, $12.00 weekends ($7.50 for 9 holes weekdays, $7.50 after 4:00 P.M. any day)

Approximate Season: April 20 to October 20

150-yard markers: Orange steel posts

Carts: Motorized and pull

Starting Times: Not available

Amenities: Full food and bar service

Telephone: 468–5581

Directions: On Route 30 three miles north of U.S. Route 4.

The Lake Bomoseen area is a summer family vacation spot with water sports, camping, hiking, and golf. Adjoining this nine-hole course is a driving range and a miniature golf course; both are open seasonally. Rooms-and-meals packages with golf included are available here. But plan to send the kids off to mini-golf or a boat ride as the card states "Children and spectators are not allowed on the course."

Most of the holes play to or from the large hill which centers this acreage on the southern end of the lake. There's a fine view from the crest of the hill where the first, fourth, and seventh greens and the second, fifth, and eighth tees converge. A swath of rough crosses the downward, sidehill second fairway and prevents you from rolling it all the way onto the green on this 155-yard par 3. The 296-yard, par-4 fourth is a real standout. The wide open fairway features a large elm tree to the right. No matter what your drive, the approach shot is blind to a large undulating green with a raised front lip. The seventh (244 yd. par 4) is also uphill, but the putting surface sits on its own plateau with a hillside behind and pot-like bunkers both right- and left-front. The 129-yard, par-3 ninth is an excellent finishing hole. A large willow tree overhangs the left side to narrow the tee shot. The pond from tee to green is an extension of Lake Bomoseen and a beautiful view is had from the front tees.

This is a short course with abundant insect life in season. But the owner-operators are friendly, the view is very Vermont, and the golf has its moments. The course is in the best condition it has ever been, with fairway grass thick and lush. The greens are small, medium speed, and very true. There is out of bounds and rough, but both are easy to avoid and thus allow a satisfying low-scoring round.

BRADFORD G.C.   Bradford

Established: 1924

Number of Holes: 9

Yardages: Middle, 4154; Forward, 4024

Par: 64

Slope: 102, 101

Fees: $10.00 weekends and weekdays

Approximate Season: May to October

150-yard markers: None

Carts: Pull carts only

Starting Times: Not necessary

Amenities: Limited food and beverage

Telephone: 222–5207

Directions: Go through downtown Bradford heading north on Route 5 and look for a right-hand turn to the course.

What looks like a flat flood plain behind downtown Bradford is really a multi-leveled nine-hole layout with quite a bit of challenge packed in to a scant 2077 yards. With the Waits River bordering the first four holes, out of bounds common, and plenty of sand traps this is certainly no pushover par 32. But the broad fairways do give everyone a chance, making Bradford a choice location for learning the game or re-sharpening old skills.

The second hole (259 yd. par 4) is a sharp, left-hand dogleg with tall trees and the river guarding the short cut to the green, which is surrounded by three good-sized traps. And the par-3 third borders the river for its entire 167 yards. A short walk up a path into the trees and you're standing on the elevated tee of the shortest golf hole in Vermont. Officially it's an 80-yard par 3, but it plays even shorter, and a trap behind the putting surface waits to grab the slightly overhit shot. Number 5 (286 yd. par 4) features out of bounds down the entire left-hand side, and a blind shot to the elevated green. The ten-foot-high embankment that fronts the green here is similar to the one in advance of the eighth green. Both have additional trouble as well—the eighth is the smallest green on the course, and the fifth is embraced by an elbow-shaped trap right and behind. The ninth (155 yards) is the fifth and final par 3 on a layout with only one par 5 and three par 4s.

If the "architect" that laid out Bradford in 1924 had seen fit to plant a few more trees in this wide field, then by now this course would have everything. As it is, they've done well with the terrain features that exist and the hazards that have been created. The fairways are thick and full, the greens small, well-groomed, and true. The sand is adequate and plentiful. Like the town of Bradford itself the club has an old-time feel to it, and more to offer than a quick look from the parking lot would reveal.

COUNTRY CLUB OF BARRE

Established: 1920s

Number of Holes: 18

Yardages: Back, 6191; Middle, 5986; Forward, 5515

Par: 71

Slope: 123, 119, 116

Fees: $10.00 with a member, $20.00 without a member (on a restricted basis) any day

Approximate Season: May to October

150-yard markers: Cedar bushes on both sides

Carts: Motorized and pull

Starting Times: Required

Amenities: Full food and bar service

Telephone: 476–7658

Directions: From Montpelier, take Route 2 east two miles past East Montpelier to Country Club Road. Go south three miles and turn left to the club.

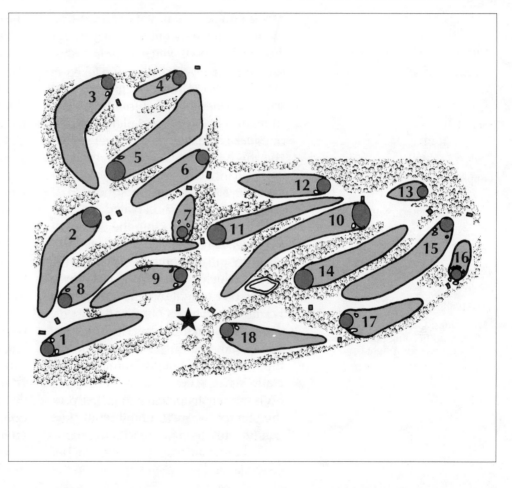

This course is almost as hard to find as it is to play. But there's a gem out there in the woods with narrow fairways, lots of deep rough, large trees, well-placed traps, undulating greens, and plenty of terrain. Add in many a blind shot, rock outcroppings, and a good physical walk, and you have enough challenge for any golfer.

The first two holes are not easy, but the first real test comes at number 3 (320 yd. par 4). From an elevated tee you must place your shot into the dogleg of a narrow fairway. Then you'll need to pitch uphill by a large tree that guards the left side of this small, fast green fronted on the right by a cloverleaf trap. The driving zone on number 8 (360 yd. par 4) is pinched by trees left, a trap, rocks, and trees right. The hole rolls gently downhill, and the same hazards are repeated green-side.

Visit the knotty-pine bar to gather your strength for the long, uphill tenth hole (525 yd. par 5). The pond and woods which border the right force play left, but go too far and you're in the trees on the hillside. Even two fine fairway shots will leave you with a delicate pitch to the sloping, plateaued green. A blind tee shot and more uphill and sidehill await on the rugged 195-yard, par-3 thirteenth. Don't try to cut any corners on number 15 (495 yd. par 5) or you'll be in the woods. Stay right and you may have a chance to see the flag on the well-trapped, hidden green to the left. Take some time on the sixteenth tee; its a great view and you can see all of this tight 135-yard par 3's pitched green surrounded by sand traps.

Barre isn't the place for someone out to duff around or learn the game of golf. But if you like "mountain golf" with plenty of problems, you'll want to find your way out here over and over again. The course is well maintained and contains flower beds and some excellent views. The holes are well separated by deep woods, and the course has not been crowded on our visits. The staff is professional and there's a small pro shop. Call ahead for starting times before heading all the way out.

KILLINGTON GOLF COURSE Sherburne

Established: 1983

Number of Holes: 18

Yardages: Back, 6326; Middle, 5896; Forward, 5664

Par: 72, 73

Slope: 134, 132, 128

Fees: $20.00 weekdays, $23.00 weekends ($15.00 after 4:00 P.M. any day)

Approximate Season: Late May to late October

150-yard markers: Gray stakes

Carts: Motorized and pull

Starting Times: Recommended

Amenities: Full food and bar service one-half mile away

Telephone: 422–3333

Directions: From the intersection of Routes 4 and 100 in Sherburne, drive about four miles up the Killington Access Road. Course is on the left—look for signs in the vicinity of Snowshed Base Lodge.

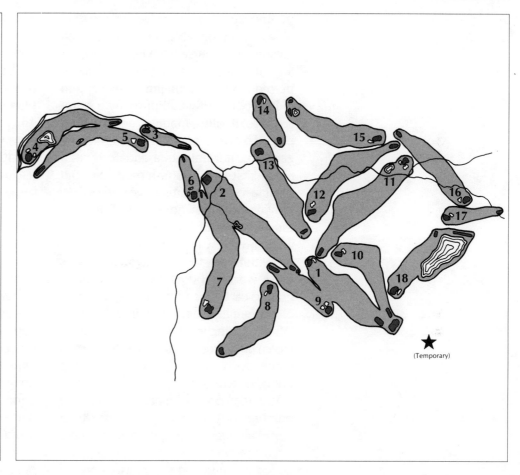

(Temporary)

One part of an extensive and growing four-season resort area, the new Killington Golf Course has a number of distinctive characteristics. Nowhere else in Vermont does the driving range happen to be a pond fully equipped with astro-turf tees, floating markers, and floating balls. The practice putting green is gargantuan and features a square central mound. Geoffrey Cornish must have had great fun with the challenge and opportunities of such mountainous terrain. Though the turf has begun to grow in well and the greens are in particularly beautiful shape for such a young course, finish work still continues. Light-rough borders can't be counted on to snag your ball before it plunges deep in the woods. What's more, you have a lot of water to face: You'll cross or play next to streams nine times, you'll encounter tiny to large ponds six times, and there's also a small wet rough area hidden front-right of number 14's green. Add in nineteen traps, all green-side (three greens are trapless), and six or seven doglegs and you have one of the most potentially punishing layouts around.

Number 2, a 485-yard par 5, proceeds sharply down from an elevated tee, possibly the greatest vertical drop of any hole in the state. You'll need both good distance and direction to reach a safe and level spot narrowed by a small pond left and trees on right. Though you might be tempted to "go for it" with shot number 2, we suggest you play for position, as a substantial area of deep rough with a rocky stream is followed by a steep bank of rough that backs up to a bilevel, trapless green.

The 163-yard, par-3 third is the most outrageous par 3 on the course and perhaps in the state. There is no fairway and no flat approach—only a hillside that begins upper left and rolls precipitously down to a stony brook running along the entire right side (see photo). There's barely enough room for the small green, never mind the cart-path collar. To make

Target golf at the 163-yard third.

hit may still leave you an uphill lie and a full pitch to clear two square traps in front. You'll want to place your ball close to the flagstick because of a ridge that divides the front and back of this medium-sized green. The 485-yard, par-5 eleventh also heads steeply down. Though this hole has a much larger landing area than number 2, stay center or slightly left to more easily cross the brook ahead on your second shot. Again, the wise will stay short for position because a barely visible pond across the brook endangers the left side and two traps embrace the front sides of this rolling green. From the back tees, number 12 (432 yd. par 4) is simply a monster. Not only is it the longest par 4, but a brook-lined gorge squarely crosses the tee-shot landing zone. Most play short and therefore take three shots to hit the green. If you're very deft or just plain daft you might go for it, otherwise play a midiron off the tee to a level spot where you'll be able to hit a fairway wood most of the way home. Even if

matters worse, the green is blind from the blue markers. The green's sloping surface does have a bunker front-right, which may just save a faded shot from the water.

Number 9 (270 yd. par 4) might sound short, but since it plays steeply uphill it feels more like 340 yards. A very good you're successful in crossing the gorge, a long blind uphill approach shot is needed to carry the right-front trap and get to the dance floor. Killington has added a new and much shorter middle tee for number 12. With 100 fewer yards than from the old middle tee, successful negotiation of the gorge becomes much more probable.

The views from Killington are exceptionally beautiful and the course itself can be extraordinarily treacherous. When it was nearly ready for play in 1983, rumor had it the carts were four-wheel drive. You may wish for one because this is definitely mountain golf and where the ski slopes end, the first tee begins.

LAKE MOREY C.C.

Established: 1915

Number of Holes: 18

Yardages: Back, 5869; Middle, 5605; Forward, 5117

Par: 70

Slope: 110, 108, 101

Fees: $16.00 weekdays, $18.00 weekends ($10.00 after 3:00 P.M. any day)

Approximate Season: May 1 to October 31

150-yard markers: White stakes

Carts: Motorized and pull

Starting Times: Recommended

Amenities: Full food and bar service

Telephone: 333–4311

Directions: Take Exit 15 on I-91. The course is on the west side of Route 5, one mile south of Fairlee.

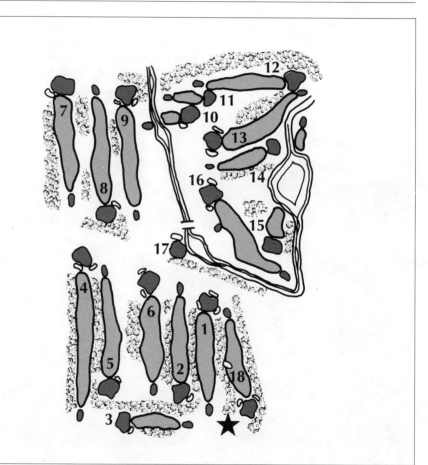

The most accessible course in the state (immediately adjacent to I–91), Lake Morey Inn and Country Club is the longtime home of the Vermont State Open. Located at the south end of the water, this course mixes a flat front nine and a hilly back nine with twenty-odd traps and water on five holes. A very walkable layout of moderately short length (there are four par 3s on the back nine), it is composed of evergreen-framed fairways and small to medium-sized greens of varying undulations and pitch.

Fairways are channeled by trees and traps along the opening holes, so the premium is on accuracy. Number 4 (475 yd. par 5) has a man-made pond carefully placed just where a faded or sliced tee shot might land. With two substantial bunkers at the green's lower front left and right, getting on in two takes more than just two big hits. The 340-yard, par-4 ninth may seem to be on the short side but it takes a very long hit to reach a view of the declivity that hides the green. A blind approach down through an opening narrowed by trees must carry two wide front traps and stop quickly on the rather small raised green. On the left there's a third trap, and the back and right borders roll off into rough. Your tee shot on the short 105-yard, par-3 tenth

The beaches of Lake Morey's ninth.

should clear a small hollow with rough and a brook to land on a little green featuring traps front and back. The highest point on the course at the thirteenth tee has a great scenic view out across the links and gives a full view of the long way down this rolling, 550-yard par 5. The fairway then narrows, dips, bends, and widens back to its eventual end at a green embraced by large front-right and back-left bunkers.

It's not too difficult to clear the brushy pond that covers much of the downhill 192 yards of par-3 number 15 if you've hit the right club. What *is* tough is the narrowness of the approach to this small, raised, trapless green.

Fairways and light rough yield good lies off well-grown turf. Greens are smooth, tightly cropped, of medium speed, and seldom flat. A wide variety of recreational activities is available at the Inn and in the general area. Consequently, this is a popular and busy spot at the height of the summer. Call ahead to check on tee times.

MONTAGUE G.C.

Established: 1925

Number of Holes: 9

Yardages: Middle, 5780; Forward, 5368

Par: 68

Slope: 116, 112

Fees: $9.00 weekdays ($5.00 after 5:00 P.M.), $14.00 weekends ($7.00 after 5:00 P.M.)

Approximate Season: April 15 to November 1

150-yard markers: Disc in fairway

Carts: Motorized and pull

Starting Times: Not required

Amenities: Cold sandwiches and full bar

Telephone: 728–3806

Directions: From Main St. in Randolph, turn east onto Merchants Row. Go straight through intersection. Take a left as road bends right in front of Tranquility Nursing Home.

The town of Randolph is well served by this Pleasant St. course overlooking the Third Branch of the White River. Operating continuously since 1925, its towering maples and evergreens have grown considerably and now direct play to a more precise level. A lower level of three holes, designed by Geoffrey Cornish, adds greatly to the beauty and challenge.

The first four holes are flat and open, but they still force you to play position for a good look into the green. There's little room behind greens 2, 3, and 4. The fifth hole (428 yd. par 4) is a beauty. From the upper level's elevated tee you look down on the long fairway bordered by swamp on the slicer's side. Even a fine drive leaves you 175 yards or more to the large, forward-tilting green with traps left and right. Number 7 (147 yd.

par 3) is the last of the three holes on this isolated lower level and concludes at a small plateau green. With woods behind, the river off to the right, and a steep-faced trap in front you'll need a precise tee shot. We have seen a great blue heron from this spot but very few birdies. Stay left on both 8 and 9 unless you enjoy scrambling down steep embankments to find an unplayable ball.

The greenskeeping crew does a thorough job at Montague and the greens have been especially smooth, fast, and true in recent years. The clubhouse is large and comfortable with cold food available. There is an active league and the course may be closed Tuesday, Wednesday, and Thursday afternoons after 3:30. Call ahead, or try a weekday morning and you might have the place to yourself.

Established: 1903

Number of Holes: 9

Yardages: Back, 5326; Middle, 5158; Forward, 4920

Par: 70

Slope: 114, 113, 110

Fees: $10.00 weekdays, $12.00 weekends

Approximate Season: April 15 to November 15

150-yard markers: Red stakes on left side

Carts: Motorized and pull

Starting Times: Not available

Amenities: Full food and bar service

Telephone: 223–7457

Directions: From the center of Montpelier, drive 1½ miles east on Route 2. Course is on left; watch for sign.

Cruising up the driveway to the Montpelier Country Club you get the impression of a few greens sliced into a large, sloping field with a huge clubhouse at the bottom. While your impression of the Elks facility may be correct, you'll have to put on your spikes and grab your clubs to know this short, older, and somewhat challenging hillside course.

The only water on the course intersects the first hole about 250 yards out and it's possible to roll a great tee shot right into it. This is also the longest par 4 and requires a lengthy second shot that avoids the flanking front traps. The third is a 430-yard uphill par 5 with woods bordering the right side and with a fast, narrow, steeply plateaued green. You may find it easy to get close in two but difficult to salvage par, as a fine touch is needed around this crowned green. This par 5 is followed by another (464-yard number 4) which features rolling sidehill terrain that hides the green until your short downhill approach shot. Number 6 is a downhill par 3 that plays quite differently on the front (146 yards) than on the back (with different tees, 204 yards) as number 15. The par-3 eighth also plays downhill over 193 yards, but rolling mounds hide the front of the green from your view. If the pin is cut in the back you may see it.

The Elks are known for their enjoyment of food and drink, and believe me, they have room to let loose here. The building that houses the golf shop, bar, and function rooms covers more acreage than some par 3s, and prices are reasonable. But there's reason to visit for the golf as well. Fairways are broad, but green-side bunkers narrow approaches. There is interesting terrain on every hole that compensates for short par 4s and 5s. The par 3s are long and tough. The greens are excellent and very quick. There's also good hole-to-hole isolation and several attractive flower beds for visual enjoyment.

RALPH MYHRE GOLF COURSE Middlebury College

Established: 1978

Number of Holes: 18

Yardages: Back, 6379; Middle, 6014; Forward, 5309

Par: 71

Slope: 129, 126, 120

Fees: $17.00 ($9.50 after 4:00 P.M.) any day

Approximate Season: May through October

150-yard markers: Squared-off yew trees

Carts: Motorized and pull

Starting Times: Recommended weekends and holidays

Amenities: Light food service, no alcoholic beverages

Telephone: 388–3711, ext. 5125

Directions: Take Route 30 southwest about one mile from Middlebury town center. Watch for sign; take a rather sudden left turn at crest of hill.

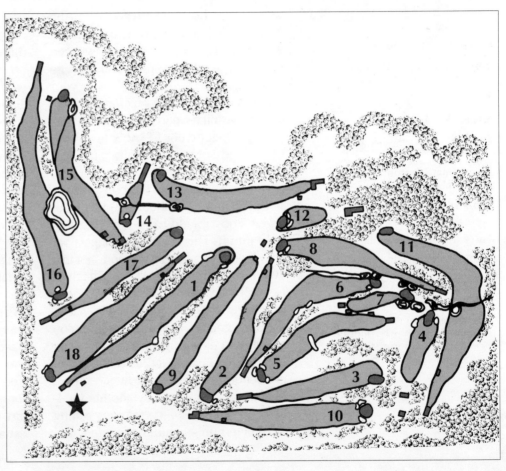

Adjacent to and part of Middlebury College, the Ralph Myhre Golf Course is laid out over the gently rolling terrain of the Champlain Valley. The casual, friendly atmosphere is as welcome as the generally wide open and forgiving fairways; but make sure your golf diploma is in your bag for your approach shots to the well-guarded greens. Traps with real sand and narrow landing areas are your mid-term, subtly undulating plateau greens the final exam. The course has been quietly well maintained on all of our visits, though early spring players may find portions wet.

The first hole is a 480-yard par 5. Straightforward and rated the least difficult handicap hole, it's our idea of the best start to a course, especially under crowded conditions. The fifth hole (370 yd. par 4) is your first dogleg; a trap and trees on the left call for a more carefully placed tee shot than appears at first glance. Companion number 6 (375 yd. par 4) doglegs right back along number 5. With only a slight difference in yardage, it nonetheless seems to play much longer. Water, water everywhere around 145-yard number 7's green; there's no sand here but a large mound front-right. Number 11 (540 yd. par 5) is rightfully the number one handicap hole. The elevated tee might help you with some distance on your drive, but watch out for a lateral water hazard that crosses the fairway 250 yards out before the dogleg is reached. A small pond graces the nearer left-hand side for those tempted to cut. If you've stayed right you may be able to fire down the dogleg to the still-hidden green. You'll find it eventually—tucked in among the trees on the right! Number 14 is a beautifully laid out, 140-yard par 3. A narrow tree-lined take-off from an elevated tee leads out over deep rough and water to a small green perched on a hillside. Fronted by a trap, it's backed up by rock outcroppings and more sloping rough. Number 15 is 380 yards of sloping dogleg with water on either side that also

The rock-faced hillside behind the fourteenth green adds to the trouble.

makes a sneaky cut across the fairway. Sheer length and a shared (but hidden) pond with 15 give 16 (535 yd. par 5) its challenge. At 410 yards, 18 is the longest par 4, and it has an additional difficulty: large trees directly in line on the fairway front the last few yards before the uphill sweep to the green.

The Myhre Course has seldom been crowded on our visits, though it has the easy accessibility of a municipal-type course. While allowing a more casual tee shot than many courses, approaches to greens should be studied carefully. The rolling terrain is used to full advantage, yielding a sturdy but walkable course with good hole-to-hole separation. This course will not yield all its pars easily and thus keeps you primed for a return to its hallowed holes!

NESHOBE G.C.   Brandon

Established: 1959

Number of Holes: 9

Yardages: Middle, 5575; Forward, 5191

Par: 71

Slope: 120, 117

Fees: $11.00 weekdays, $13.00 weekends

Approximate Season: Early April through October

150-yard markers: Brown stakes

Carts: Motorized and pull

Starting Times: Not available

Amenities: Full food and bar service

Telephone: 247-3611

Directions: From Brandon travel just over a mile east on Route 73. Take a left onto Country Club Road to the clubhouse.

The Neshobe Golf Club can be counted on as one of the first courses in the state to open for play each spring. This alone is enough to bring out the faithful from winter's fold to the gentle hills and willow-lined fairways that play along the quiet Neshobe River. Good use has been made of what nature provided: this single stream affects play on seven of the nine holes. Serviceable fairways, very playable light rough, fourteen bunkers and greens of moderate speed complete the picture of a course that appeals to a wide range of players.

Not one par 4 is over 375 yards, and number 7 is well under at 272 yards. From an elevated tee, a flat fairway leads straight to a large trap centered at the base of a steady upsweep of rough. The hole is open on the right save for a few trees, but a dense thicket guards the steeper left side. Stay short of all the trouble by playing a long iron to allow a precise wedge up to the hidden rectangular green.

Two sets of tees add variety by creating a second nine holes. For instance, a second teeing ground changes number 8 from a 192-yard par 3 into the 268-yard, par-4 seventeenth. The challenge comes first from the river which crosses just in front of the green, and second from a large tree just off the green to the left.

The atmosphere is casual here though the course can be quite busy. Popular with many area residents, it's a fine spot for an outing with friends or family. A good place for an introduction to the game, Neshobe can challenge the weekend golfer without suspending enjoyment.

Established: 1927

Number of Holes: 9

Yardages: Back, 5902; Middle, 5728; Forward, 4828

Par: 70, 68

Slope: 119, 115, 109

Fees: $10.00 weekdays, $15.00 weekends

Approximate Season: April 15 to October 15

150-yard markers: Green and white stakes

Carts: Motorized and pull

Starting Times: Recommended weekends

Amenities: Full food and bar service

Telephone: 485–4515

Directions: Two miles south of Northfield Center on Roxbury Road.

Northfield C.C. is a rural course with a variety of terrains just a little off the beaten path. A casual, low-key atmosphere yields a comfortable feel that belies what some might expect at the "typical" country club. Recent modifications to the well-grown-in course have substantially improved playability in recent years.

The Dog River figures prominently in your plans to par the opening two holes, which share a large field for their fairways. Your approach shot on number 2 (already the third crossing of the river) is particularly tight due to trees and sand. After the short third hole, cross the road to reach the fourth tee and the rest of the course. Yes, there is a small hidden green on top of that sizable mound: it's all uphill carry on this 165-yard par 3. Choose your iron carefully because if your ball doesn't stop on the green you're looking at bogey plus. The 368-yard, par-4 fifth is a chameleon hole that becomes a par 5 of 467 yards as number 14. Your tee shot must carry a rolling gorge and stay right to afford a view of the green. The 537-yard, par-5 sixth—the number 1 handicap hole—will have you out on the railroad tracks if you pull your distance shots in an attempt to avoid the undulating and rolling right side. The green on 6 has been completely rebuilt and is now fronted by a treacherously deep trap. The new tee for the 320-yard, par-4 seventh is now just behind the sixth green, providing higher elevation and a long-shot chance to cut a corner over the Dog River. The 178-yard, par-3 eighth features a rocky waste area in center fairway that hides your landing area on the mound-encircled green.

Back at the clubhouse relax with an inexpensive brew out on the front porch and think about how you'll par number 4 next visit. Though the course has been completely revised since its opening in 1927, it has a mature feel. The ball sits up well in both fairway and rough, and greens roll fair and true. Since this course is out of the way and busy at times, it's best to call ahead.

Established: 1927

Number of Holes: 18

Yardages: Middle, 5721; Forward, 5530

Par: 70, 72

Slope: 125, 123

Fees: $12.00 weekdays, $14.00 weekends

Approximate Season: May to October 31

150-yard markers: Posts on the side of some fairways

Carts: Motorized and pull

Starting Times: Not available

Amenities: Full food and bar service

Telephone: 483-9379

Directions: Take Route 7 north from center Rutland. About three miles from town, turn left on Cedar Ave. just after the Nissan dealer. Turn right on N. Grove St. and go 2½ miles. Club is on right at top of rise.

Recently cited in the USGA publication *Golf Journal* for its unique marble clubhouse, Proctor-Pittsford sits atop a hill looking towards the Green Mountain National Forest. Built in 1927 by the Vermont Marble Company, the course features uniform rows of oak, pine, cedar, and willows lining nearly every fairway. Those and a substantial amount of out of bounds work to narrow forty to seventy yard-wide fairways. But long hitters will still have many wedge shots to par 4s as short as 278 yards.

In 1989 the club will further distinguish itself in the eyes of the golfing world. F. Ray Keyser, Jr., a club member and former governor of Vermont, has designed a new back nine. Tree lined, with varied terrain and views of the picturesque town of Proctor, this acreage will enhance anyone's golfing experience at Proctor-Pittsford. The new holes will open when weather permits in 1989.

While there are no flat holes at Proctor-Pittsford, number 6 (384 yd. par 4) is the sharpest downhill and number 7 the steepest up. Number 6 has six of the course's twenty-six sand traps. Aim your drive at the bunker visible beyond the fairway if you can hit it 230 yards or more. Otherwise you won't have a clear shot around the left-hand dogleg. Sand surrounds the green, with woods and water beyond. The fairway on 7 may be 70 yards wide, but it's still 487 yards of uphill par 5. A small pond in front of the ladies' tee used to be accompanied by a large pine tree (now deceased) that split the fairway. When you eventually chug up to the green you'll find it slanted, bi-level, very quick, and hugged by a trap on the right—perfect for three putting.

Fairways here are thick and full and the ball sits up well. Approach areas bounce true but hard, and the greens themselves are medium fast. The back nine is a close match and in ten years you'll scarcely know the difference between the two nines. Stay out of the sand that pesters you on nearly every hole and away from the rows of trees and you'll score well.

THE QUECHEE CLUB

Established: 1970 (Lakeland), 1975 (Highland)

Number of Holes: 36

Yardages: Highland: Back, 6765; Middle, 6341; Forward, 5439

Lakeland: Back, 6103; Middle, 5627; Forward, 5061

Par: 72 (Highland), 70 (Lakeland)

Slope: Highland: 129, 123, 119; Lakeland: 128, 124, 117

Note: See text to see who may play here and when

Approximate Season: May 1 to November 1

150-yard markers: Brown stakes

Carts: Motorized and pull

Starting Times: Recommended

Amenities: Full food and bar service

Telephone: 295–6245

Directions: From Quechee Village just off Route 4 follow River Road northwest about one mile.

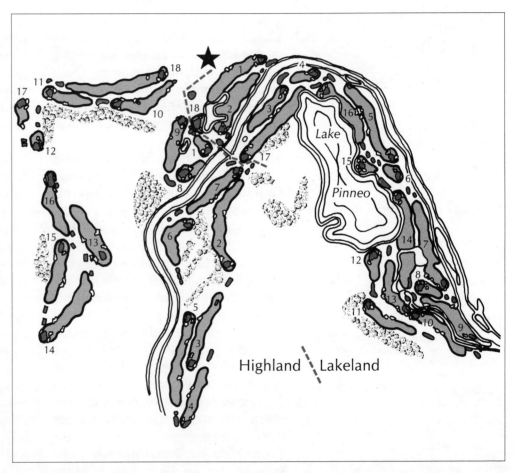

Quechee Lakes Corporation has in the extensive development of the area built two adjacent and outstanding Geoffrey Cornish-designed layouts. Now semi-private, play is limited to members, guests, and tenants with the special exception of Vermont Lung Card holders and those competing in the New England Open. While both courses have numerous large, deep, carefully placed traps, lush carpet-like fairways, and very fast greens, each has its own character. Lakeland, considerably shorter, has water hazards on some seventeen holes and, frequently, narrow landing and approach areas. Highland has length and terrain in full measure.

The Highland course is considered one of the very best courses in the region and among the top 1 percent in the country according to *Golf Digest*. It also has the second highest course rating in the state—73.1 from the blue tees. Trees line the fairway on the higher left side of 421-yard number 3, the longest par 4. That's the side to aim along because the pitch will carry anything hit center or right into right-hand rough or a trap-faced mound. Further up on the right a saddle-shaped trap straddles another mound, yielding trouble on both sides for holes 3 and 5. A gaping trap front-right and green-side will keep you to the left as you run your approach shot down the contours. Number 8 (241 yards from blue and 221 yards from white) is the longest par 3 on either course—and in the state—but that's not all. Your tee shot must carry 170 yards over the rippling waters of the Ottauquechee River to bounce onto the large, undulating green, which is surrounded by big multi-lobed traps and mounds. The back nine continues with a particularly beautiful series of holes; especially notable are par 3s 12 and 17, which share a deep ravine. 175-yard number 12, while somewhat more open, is all carry up a steep slope that has two large traps set into the left side. Close by the left of this flat, medium-sized green is out of bounds, and along the tree-lined right the cart

The break in the trees in the distance is the tee for the seventeenth at Quechee Highlands.

path itself is a factor. Number 17 (190 yd. par 3) plays back across deep woods from a very elevated tee. Visible in the distance is the upsweep to a large green with traps right-front, back, and left, all closely framed by trees.

Avoiding water is a top priority on the Lakeland course. On the 382-yard, par-4 second the river runs the length of the left side, and a pond green-side right greatly narrows your approach. Your tee shot on number 3 (345 yd. par 4) must travel across the river and through a field goal of trees to the fairway. There you'll have a downhill shot that must clear a yawning trap set just in front of the small, sloping green. The Ottauquechee River continues to haunt your left side out to the turn and man-made Lake Pinneo complicates the left again on the way back home.

Geoffrey Cornish reviewed the Lakeland course and substantial changes were made in 1987. Number 1 was lengthened with a new tee (and carry over water), and number 11 was completely remodeled into a long par 5 with green-side ponds. A new par-4 twelfth turned the old number 12 into the new number 13 and so on down the line. The old par-3 eighteenth was dropped from the card. Completed in August 1988, Lakeland is now a par 72 with water on 17 of the 18 holes.

There's more top-quality golf here than anywhere else in the state and thus a wider variety of problems to solve.

Though the exclusive nature of the Quechee Club may make it difficult to get on, it's well worth a try through the various possibilities listed. Both courses offer golf challenges well beyond the average, so bring your best game.

RUTLAND C.C.

Established: 1902

Number of Holes: 18

Yardages: Back, 6062; Middle, 5761; Forward, 5368

Par: 70, 71

Slope: 129, 127, 121

Fees: $20.00 with a member, $30.00 without a member any day

Approximate Season: April 15 to October 31

150-yard markers: Plates in fairway, bushes on both sides

Carts: Motorized and pull

Starting Times: Required

Amenities: Full food and bar service

Telephone: 773–3254

Directions: Merchants Row downtown becomes Grove Street. Follow it north 1½ miles; course is on left.

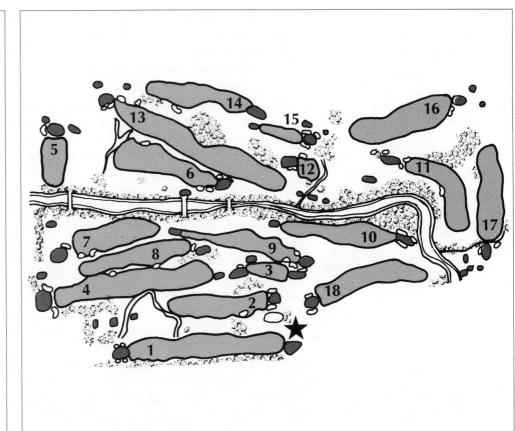

How can 5854 yards be this tough you ask? How can the white course rating be only 68.5 when average golfers score in the upper 90s? Well, course ratings don't take difficult terrain into account* and Rutland's got some of that. And total yardages don't tell you anything about small slippery slanted greens, and Rutland's got some of those. And neither figure would warn you about forty-five green-side sand traps, but they're also there. In short, Rutland C.C. provides a fine examination of your golf game. With little concentration on length, Rutland tests your putting skills. If you love fast greens go there on a warm day in August.

The course features four excellent, diverse, and demanding par 3s. The 145-yard third will reward only a perfect shot with a putt for birdie. A medium-small green angles away from you, and an elbow trap waits like a moat around the right and front. An embank-

*But see Appendix B for the latest on the new Slope System, which does take into account such factors.

ment falls in sharply from the left, broken only by a large rock face a few yards off the green. The green itself is slanted and contoured. The 232-yard, par-3 fifth is a whole 'nother kettle of fish. Here's one of the longest par 3s in the state and it's all carry. The tee overlooks East Creek and then rises in three steps to a plateaued green. A trap left may save a long draw from going out of bounds, but the right front of the carpet could reject a slight fade back down into the fairway. The strategy here: hit all you've got and then make it stop quick and hold.

There are problems on the layout's twelve par 4s as well. Drive only to the end of the flat on the 360-yard, par-4 sixth. A shot beyond will yield a downhill lie from which to hit your second into a dangerously fast small green with sneaky sand everywhere. And don't hit all you've got from the tee at 11 (324 yd. par 4) or you may clear the fairway. This left-hand dogleg concludes at a green trapped front and back and only twelve yards wide. The 200-yard, par-3 twelfth

Rutland C.C. features slippery sloping greens and numerous nearby traps.

includes a trap nearly as large as the green. It's directly adjacent on the left but down a seven-foot embankment. Besides that, there's not a flat spot on or around the green (or anywhere but the tee for that matter). At least the final par 3 is the shortest. At only 130 yards, and with a tee elevated twenty-five feet above the green, number 15 requires a very soft shot. Try to run it up and it'll run into the trap on the right that everything tilts into. The green on number 16 (363 yd. par 4) typifies the Rutland layout. More sloped than undulating, it's swift with no easy pin placements. Stay below the pin here as elsewhere and try to get your first putt close.

The original nine at Rutland was designed by George Low, runner-up in the 1899 U.S. Open and professional at Baltusrol in New Jersey and Ekwanok in Manchester. The Rutland Golf Club had purchased the 382-acre Baxter Farm for $4,648 in 1902 and continued to operate it as both a farm and a club for years. In 1927 Wayne Stiles remodeled the existing nine, keeping five holes mostly intact, and added another nine. The new and present layout opened on May 1, 1928, and has seen little revision since, save for the planting of ornamental trees and bushes. Even with modern-age golf equipment the course remains an excellent test. The ball sits up well in close-clipped fairways, and behaves as expected from uniform beach-like sand. The back nine not only features several difficult greens, but great aesthetics with its beautiful hillside landscapes and views to the Pico-Killington range.

SUGARBUSH G.C. Warren

Established: 1963

Number of Holes: 18

Yardages: Back, 6524; Middle, 5886; Forward, 5187

Par: 72, 70, 72

Slope: 128, 122, 114

Fees: $25.00 ($20.00 after 3:00 P.M.) any day

Approximate Season: May 15 to October 15

150-yard markers: Red-topped stakes and yellow plates in mid-fairway

Carts: Motorized and pull

Starting Times: Recommended

Amenities: Full food and bar service

Telephone: 583–2722

Directions: Travel four miles south of Waitsfield on Route 100, then turn right onto the Sugarbush Ski Area access road. Drive about a mile and look for a sign and a left turn. Proceed another mile to the clubhouse.

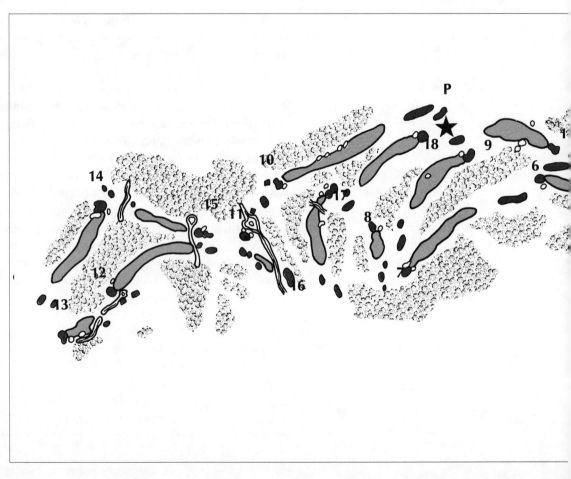

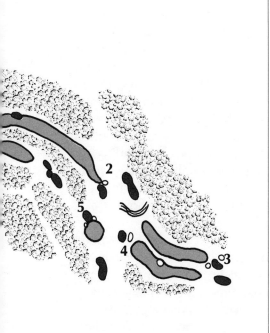

The Sugarbush Golf Club is part of the extensive and beautiful four-season resort area of Waitsfield-Warren. The course itself nestles in along hillsides that quickly rise up into ski slopes. This is no bunny-slope beginners' run here, but one of the longest and most difficult courses in the state. Par or near-par golf is hard won; the Robert Trent Jones design makes the most of very mountainous terrain. Narrow fairways and thirty-two traps create a demand for both length and accuracy. Furthermore, there are only one or two holes anywhere close to being flat, and the inevitable blind shots are caused by the terrain itself as much as by doglegs.

Number 2, a 548-yard par 5 from the blue tees, while not the longest par 5, is nevertheless rated the toughest of the four. From a very elevated tee, the fairway begins heading right and continues thus most of the way to the green. Deep rough, rocks, and trees line the drop-off on the left-side; rock outcroppings, more deep rough, and trees rise on the right. From a hillside lie, your second shot will hopefully reach the flatter and wider approach-shot zone. When you've managed to reach this more forgiving area, you may still have a solid midiron to get you up a short rise to the medium-sized rolling green trapped front-left. At the 435-yard, par-4 seventh, those who used the white tees might wish for the blue: the extra 25 yards (460 yards) creates a par 5. And you may need that extra stoke because your long blind second shot must carry the hillcrest and move down sharply to a medium-sized green closely guarded by traps front right and left. Back and right it drops off quickly, and the left side before and along the green is tightly tree lined.

Number 11 (115 yd. par 3) is 100 percent target shooting. From an elevated tee you'll see deep rough downhill to a pond and a narrow trap left on a short roll-up. The small and shallow green is set into a wooded hillside. Number 14 (470 yd. par 5) starts off from an elevated tee and calls for a fairway wood into a wide-open fairway elbow area. Here the hole turns left and runs downhill all the long way to a full-sized green. A strategic pond is set just in the front left and center, a small green-side trap lies off to the right, and once again the back slopes off into woods. The 178-yard, par-3 sixteenth is graced with one of the larger greens of the layout—a very good thing because it's another target shot. A rocky stream-lined gorge crosses the far end of

A long second shot is required to clear the hidden pond before the twelfth green.

a short sloping fairway before the quick rise up to the green; fortunately, there is a little room either side of the green and back, and no sand.

On return visits, we've told ourselves that because it's midsummer and we're playing well and we know the course— today we score. It's never happened. This course has the capability of bringing just about anybody to their knees. Your first visit may be confounding and befuddling; if you walk it, fatigue will be a factor. Treat any par as precious and expect to rack up a few more strokes than is customary.

The light rough can be quite deep. Though generally full and thick, fairways may dry out in late summer. The medium-to-fast greens are seemingly always pitched, never flat, and the subtle undulations frequently make careful readings mandatory. (We swear the ball will break uphill when putted on certain locations of the eighteenth green.) This beautiful and challenging layout will make you want to return again and again to attempt a better score. Good luck!

Established: 1972

Number of Holes: 9

Yardage: Middle, 5600

Par: 70, 74

Slope: 100, 98

Fees: $10.00 weekdays, $12.00 weekends ($5.00 after 4:30 P.M. any day)

Approximate Season: April to November

150-yard markers: None

Carts: Pull carts only

Starting Times: Not necessary

Amenities: Soda machine only

Telephone: 767–3709

Directions: Course is halfway between Stockbridge and Rochester on the west side of Route 100.

If you're looking for the most laid-back course in the state, or maybe the flattest, or both, come on down to the large red barn south of Rochester that serves as the pro shop for the White River Golf Club. Originally operated as a course in the 1920s, then abandoned to dairy farming, it was resurrected in 1971 and opened the following year to the delight of local duffers. The layout occupies a fertile piece of flood plain between Route 100 and the First Branch of the White River, and it opens for practice as soon as weather allows (early February one snowless winter).

The fourth hole (285 yd. par 4) is bordered by trees and the river on the right the entire length of the fairway, and plays to a contoured green. The fifth, a 133-yard par 3, is framed by large trees with a small stream running through the fairway and a green tilted away from you. The eighth hole, at 427 yards, is by far the longest par 4. A small rise shortly after the tee makes your drive a blind one. The green sits in front of some woods with the White River rolling close by on the right.

Don't come to the White River G.C. to practice your sand shots (there is no sand) or your putting (the greens need some work). You may even want to bring a picnic lunch as there's very little food available. But there is plenty of room to practice from the tees and well-kept fairways. In fact, this is one of the better places in the state to learn the game of golf. The views of the nearby mountains in the Rochester area are outstanding. And there might not be a better course for bird watching—a brief visit one spring featured sightings of hawks, small water birds, and even an osprey cruising the river environs.

WOODSTOCK C.C.

Established: 1896

Number of Holes: 18

Yardages: Back, 6001; Middle, 5555; Forward, 4956

Par: 69, 71

Slope: 121, 117, 109

Fees: $35.00 ($16.00 after 4:00 P.M.) any day

Approximate Season: Early May to early October

150-yard markers: Brown posts on either side

Carts: Motorized and pull

Starting Times: Recommended

Amenities: Full food and bar service

Telephone: 457–2114

Directions: One mile south of the Woodstock green on the east side of Route 106.

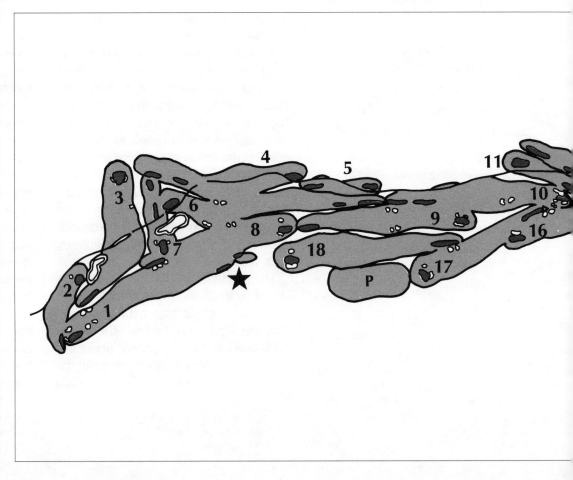

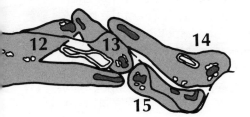

The Woodstock Country Club is unique in Vermont for several reasons: It has the most beautiful and least forgiving sand traps because Rock Resorts flew in white sand from Bermuda when the course was remodeled by Robert Trent Jones in 1963. It is one of the most meticulously maintained courses, yet done so in a way that rarely interferes with play. It may occupy the least acreage of any eighteen-hole layout, and yet it still finds room for an excellent practice area with putting green, driving range, and a separate chipping green with sand trap. Its architectural evolution has been shaped by many famous names including William Tucker (1906), Walter Travis (1912), Wayne Stiles (1924), Donald Ross (1930s), and R.T. Jones. And finally, it has one of the strictest dress codes of any public course: no cutoffs, blue jeans, jogging shorts, t-shirts, fishnet shirts, or tank tops.

The course itself is fairly flat and rather short, putting a high premium on accuracy. Kedron Brook, with its ten-foot embankments, winds through or along twelve of the eighteen holes, and it must be negotiated twice on holes 4 and 12. You cross it first on number 3 (346 yd. par 4). If you've been here before and can hit a long draw you'll clear it with no problem. In any case your second shot will be blindly uphill to a mounded green bordered by evergreens and nearby out of bounds. The elevated tee on number 4 (382 yd. par 4) looks down across the tree-lined brook to a very small landing zone. Twin fairway traps with dense pine trees lie just beyond. And that ideal area is still 180 yards from the putting surface, which is embraced by the brook again. The Kedron isn't as much of a factor on the scenic 162-yard, par-3 seventh, but the pond, traps, and trees are, making proper club selection and straight, accurate shooting vital. Not surprisingly, water is a factor on all three of the par 3s on the back side. It seems the least threatening on number 13 (150 yd.) but has unexpectedly snagged many a fade bounding off the right side mound

Keeping it from the Kedron River is your aim at Woodstock.

pin-high. The twelfth (381 yd. par 4) is very similar to the double-brook crossing of number 4, with a tad more room to miss the green short (which helps you avoid finding your ball down with the trout).

There is fairness and consistency in this course design, and even the short hitter who can keep it out of the brook can score well. Carpetlike fairways are open, but approaches are tight, and inches are the difference between pars and a sand-trap triple-bogey nightmare. With little up and down, it's an easy walk and can be enjoyed by players of all abilities. Of all the public courses in Vermont, Woodstock C.C. feels the most like you're an invited guest to a private club. Bring your best golf etiquette, a working sand wedge, and an extendible ball retriever.

SOUTH

Established: 1927

Number of Holes: 9

Yardages: Middle, 5807; Forward, 5292

Par: 70, 72

Slope: 114, 109, 106

Fees: $8.00 for 9 holes, $10.00 for 18 holes weekdays; $12.00 for 9 holes, $14.50 for 18 holes weekends ($6.50 after 5:00 P.M. weekdays, $8.50 after 3:00 P.M. weekends)

Approximate Season: April 1 to November 1

150-yard markers: Small bushes

Carts: Motorized and pull

Starting Times: Not available

Amenities: Light food and full bar

Telephone: 463–9809

Directions: About three miles north on Route 103 from Exit 6 off I-91 (across from the Vermont Country Store).

An older course which has been re-modeled extensively, Bellows Falls C.C. is an interesting layout whose challenge comes not from length but from numerous blind shots. The reason: terrain that varies from rolling to very hilly and is always a factor. Though there are visible landing areas they are usually small; larger ones are either hidden or pitched, yielding a diversity of lies on the well-groomed fairways. Light rough tends to be open and playable especially in the tree-lined borders dividing adjacent holes. The small and medium-sized greens are of an average speed with some appreciably faster.

At 525 yards, par-5 number 2 offers more than just a long and hilly stretch of open fairway. Even two long woods will leave you wondering where the green is on your first visit here. Though blind, your approach shot is actually not that tough because you'll be hitting to a bunkerless seventeen by twenty-five-yard green that occupies the bottom of a grassy bowl over twenty feet deep.

Par-3 number 4 is 163 yards and 97 percent is carry. A deep declivity separates the tee from a hidden green set up on a somewhat higher plateau. The two traps behind it save the long ball from a steep drop-off into the woods. Number 5 (341 yd. par 4) has one of the smallest greens of any hole in the state, and the well-placed trap behind it snags the inevitably overhit second shot. On the 318 yard, par-4 seventh, stay short of the sharp 18-foot step-up in mid-fairway. It's a blind second shot to the small green that is three-quarters encircled by a long skinny trap. Beautifully set and mounded green-side bunkers, as well as the blind uphill drive, complicate the 437-yard, par-5 ninth, but an eagle putt is not inconceivable here.

Just driving by on Route 103 you wouldn't realize what excellent use the hidden terrain has been put to. Watch for a generic "Golf Course" sign which points you to a relaxed and unpretentious clubhouse.

BRATTLEBORO C.C.

Established: 1914

Number of Holes: 9

Yardages: Middle, 5950; Forward, 5815

Par: 71

Slope: 117, 108

Note: Residents of Brattleboro and bordering towns can play only as members or guests of members. There is no play available for the general public on weekends, holidays, or Fridays after 11:30 A.M.

Fees: $10.00 for 9 holes, $14.00 for 18 holes weekdays; $12.00 for 9 holes, $16.00 for 18 holes weekends.

Approximate Season: May to October 31

Starting Times: Required

Amenities: Full food and bar service

Telephone: 257–7380

Directions: Take Route 9 west from Exit 2 of I-91. Turn right on Orchard St. across from Texaco station. Go 1½ miles and bear right. Turn right again on to Dummerston Road and right once more into the club.

In December 1913 Tom McNamara, a Boston golf pro, laid out a nine-hole course on the current site of the Brattleboro C.C. The layout was rearranged, and a few holes changed entirely by Wayne Stiles in later years. It has now evolved into a well-balanced course in which each hole is interesting and presents more than the usual amount of problems to the average golfer. The traps were all resculpted and refilled with deep, fluffy sand in late 1986. The greens, small to medium in size, are quick, uniform, and true. There are blind shots, small prime landing zones, and greenside mounding: all contribute to the second-highest course rating (70) of any nine-holer in Vermont.

Although out of bounds borders the right side of the first four holes, it comes into play the most on tilted number 3, a 505-yard par 5. Narrowed by trees left and the roadside out of bounds right, this rolling hole is complicated by a blind second shot and green-side bunkers just a few feet and a short drop off the putting surface. The fourth hole is a steadily uphill par 4 of 380 yards. A good solid drive will still leave 175 more uphill yards to a green that faces the fairway and echoes its slope. The carpet is larger than some here but has fewer easy pin placements. The fifth (385 yd. par 4) may be the toughest test yet. The prime landing zone is a tiny area of fairway left and long. Only there will you see a portion of this small green set into the edge of the woods. From the right side of the avenue you'll be looking at a small hill that juts into the fairway and is capped by a large maple tree. With traps protecting the only bail-out area left of the green, par from here would be well earned. A precise tee shot is also the ticket to a par 4 on the 345-yard eighth. A long slight fade aimed at fairway center would avoid mounding on both sides and maybe carry down to the flat approach lane. Be careful of that left-front trap, the guardian maple tree right, and absolutely nothing but thin air behind the green's left rear.

CROWN POINT C.C.

Established: 1953

Number of Holes: 18

Yardages: Back, 6572; Middle, 6120; Forward, 5542

Par: 72

Slope: 123, 119, 114

Fees: $26.00 ($10.00 after 5:00 P.M.) any day

Approximate Season: April 15 to October 31

150-yard markers: Small evergreens

Carts: Motorized and pull

Starting Times: Recommended

Amenities: Full food and bar service

Telephone: 885–2703

Directions: Two and a half miles north of Springfield out Elm Street. Course on west side of Weathersfield Center Road.

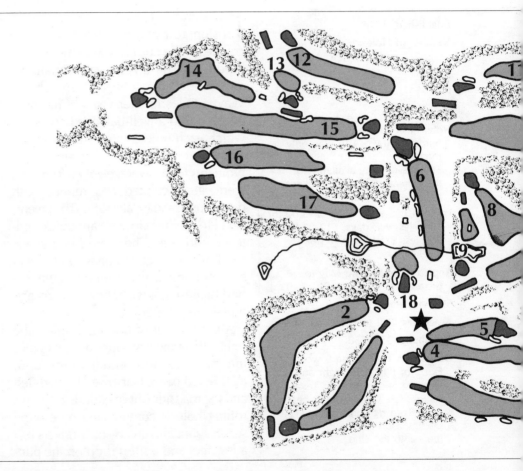

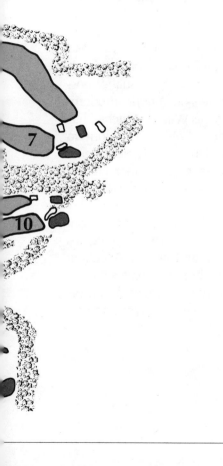

The site of the 1983 New England Amateur, Crown Point has all the elements of a championship golf course and a touch of Revolutionary War history as well. The Crown Point Military Road, built in 1760 to link Fort Number 4 in Charlestown, N.H., with Fort Ticonderoga, passes by the tenth green. The entire course straddles a ridge line that provides plenty of hilly terrain for nearly every hole. Well groomed and seldom crowded, Crown Point rewards the well-placed shot while providing enough room for the casual golfer to duff around.

The first five holes, which lie between the club house and the road, warm you up for the fun, which begins with number 6, an uphill 365-yard dogleg par 4. Your best tee shot will still leave you well below a bunkered green. Don't try to cut the corner or you may just hop into one of three strategically placed fairway traps. The seventh (487 yd. par 5) runs along the crest of the ridge with a crowned fairway that deflects off-center tee shots to either side. A mound on the right and a trap to the left complicate your approach to this backless green. Number 8 (376 yd. par 4) is a sharp right-hand dogleg where the second shot is uphill and blind over a large rock outcropping. When you eventually climb up there you'll find the green—the flattest part of the hole—framed by trees.

The back side begins with a series of five outstanding holes. The tenth is 344 yards of sidehill lies that finish to a fast, pitched bilevel green. Number 11 (463 yd. par 5) would take two great shots for an eagle putt. Center your drive down to the beginning of the fairway. Your second shot sets you up for a wedge left to an elevated green set in a steep embankment and fronted by a giant trap. Most of us are happy to be on in three. To hit the next green (390 yd. par 4) in two is an even greater accomplishment. Stay left with your tee shot and pray for your long, uphill approach to hold the slick, small putting surface. Plenty of ter-

This small shelf is your target on the 154-yard, par-3 ninth.

nabbed you, one of several around the green might.

There is an out-in-the-country feel to Crown Point due to its views of Mt. Ascutney, beautiful surrounding fields and farms, and friendly, casual atmosphere. And there's no generic, modern-day design here, as William Mitchell has created 18 unique holes that conform to the natural lay of the land. There's plenty of unused acreage, also, that creates great overall hole-to-hole isolation. Extended seasons are the rule with play beginning early in the spring and continuing until snowfall. The terrain gives good drainage, and the Connecticut River Valley location moderates the climate. A fair price, a congenial atmosphere, and an excellent layout add up to fun for all.

rain remains as number 14 (344 yd. par 4) demonstrates. Your tee shot is forced downhill and right, away from the bunkered hilltop green. If the fairway trap protecting the left-hand shortcut hasn't

EQUINOX C.C.

Established: 1927

Number of Holes: 18

Yardages: Back, 6451; Middle, 6022; Forward, 5278

Par: 71

Slope: 123, 119, 112

Fees: $22.00 weekdays, $27.00 weekends

Approximate Season: May 1 to October 15

150-yard markers: Brown posts on right side

Carts: Motorized and pull

Starting Times: Required

Amenities: Full food and bar service

Telephone: 362–3223

Directions: One hundred yards east of the Equinox Hotel in Manchester.

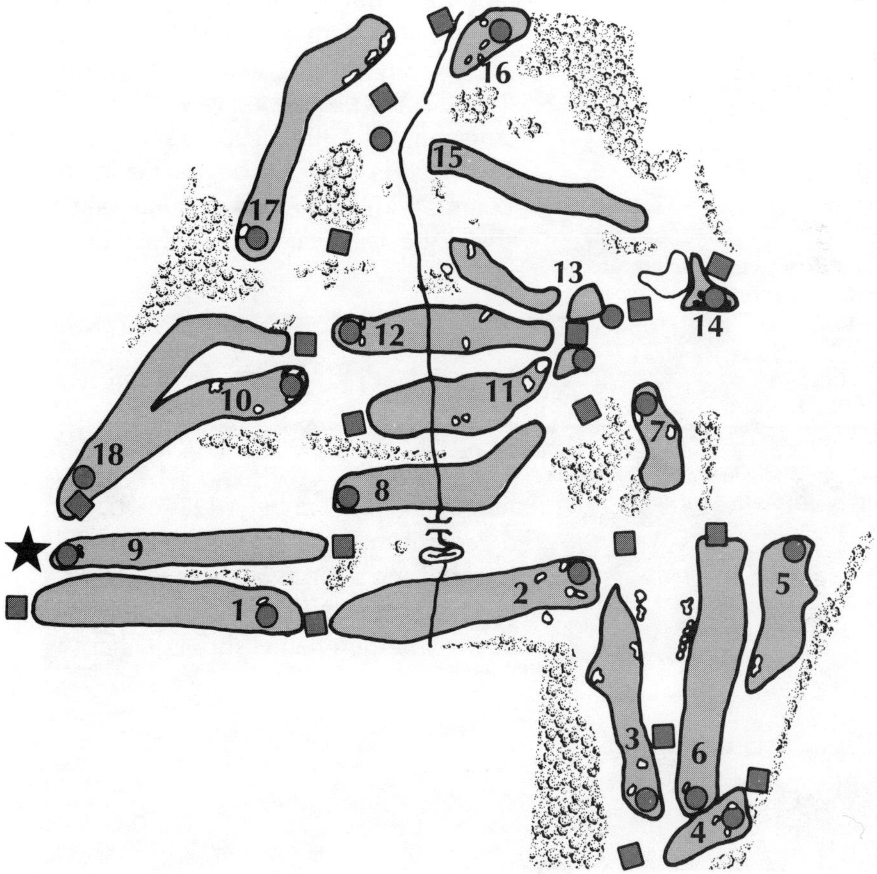

Walter Travis emigrated to the United States from Australia in 1885 at age twenty-three. Taking up golf in 1897, Travis proceeded to win the U.S. Amateur in 1900, 1901, and 1903. During this time he began designing courses with John Duncan Dunn, one of their greatest early creations being Ekwanok C.C. in Manchester. Travis returned to the area in 1927 (the year of his death) to lay out adjoining Equinox on the site of the former Hillside Golf Club, thereby reestablishing golfing grounds in use since 1894. Except for some revision by William Mitchell in 1967, the course remains intact today. The challenges of sixty years ago are still there: small greens, strategically placed sand, sneaky water, and severely contoured terrain.

After three relatively flat and open par 4s to start (each with its own problems around the green), number 4 (168 yd. par 3) is a fine placement test for that medium or long iron. Steadily uphill with woods bordering the right, it plays to a tiny bilevel green with traps on three sides. A slice will careen off a sidehill into unplayable territory and an overhit ball could clear the next tee. A slice from the fifth tee will be O.K. although you wouldn't know it standing up there. The entire hole lies unseen over a fairway mound fifty yards from the tee. From

There is difficulty everywhere around the fourteenth green.

The mounded traps between 6 and 7.

embankment is broken only by a large, deep trap. Other interesting hazards block your way back to the clubhouse—an outstanding series of fairway traps lying between 6 and 7, the stream that sneaked across number 2 interrupts the driving zone on 8, and bilevel greens on 6 and 9.

All the elements of great design come together on the awe-inspiring holes 13 through 16. Here all the hazards are laid out before you but you'll still fall prey to them. The putting surface on rolling number 13 (383 yd. par 4) sits on a pedestal forty feet above the fairway. Make sure you get there because pitching down off the steep-faced hill behind is better than pitching blindly up from the deep grass below. The fourteenth is a classic 121-yard par 3 from an elevated tee to a small green entirely surrounded by sand and pine trees. The fifteenth is a 475-yard roller coaster ride of terrain. You go from a tee on high down into a pit, then up, down, and up again. Your blind second shot on this par 5 could

there it's all downhill on this 345-yard par 4. The perfectly hit drive that hugs the trees on the left could roll all the way down to the perched green. But most of us will hit a short second from an awkward downhill lie. This shot will be drawn right, where a steep green-side

101

easily bound off the fairway into the same small stream that splits the course and haunts seven of its holes. Here it's the closest it gets to a green and it easily turns birdies into bogeys. All the sand, sidehill lies, and trees you can see from the sixteenth tee are in front of the green on this 172-yard par 3, so get the ball all the way there. The green is large and flat—for Equinox, that is.

Of all the 18-hole courses in the state, the greens at Equinox are the smallest overall. Since they are always contoured, often bilevel, and also very quick (frequently rejecting your ball), you must putt well to score. With fairway traps, blind shots, hillside lies, and old stands of trees, the course truly challenges both games of golf—that played in the air, and that on the ground. But relax and enjoy these ninety-year-old links; afterwards there's a bar with a great porch that faces a picture postcard view of the southern Green Mountains.

FOX RUN G.C.

Established: 1969

Number of Holes: 9

Yardages: Middle, 5280; Forward, 5094

Par: 70, 72

Slope: 106, 102

Fees: $10.00 for 9 holes, $16.00 for 18 holes ($7.00 after 4:00 P.M.) any day

Approximate Season: May to October

150-yard markers: Wooden posts on both sides

Carts: Motorized and pull

Starting Times: Required 24 hours in advance

Amenities: Full food and bar service

Telephone: 228–8871

Directions: On the east side of Routes 100 and 103, 1½ miles north of Ludlow.

One of several nine-hole facilities in the state planning for expansion to eighteen, Fox Run sits between hills behind Ludlow and the Black River. A couple of ponds and streams, twenty-five sand traps, and a multitude of large old trees help add some challenge to only 5187 yards.

A severe dogleg, the 327-yard, par-4 second would be a tough hole on any layout. Long hitters should use an iron on the tee, but believe it or not there's room enough for the rest of us to hit a wood. Two large fairway traps lurk just beyond the tall trees that guard the shortcut. It's not much more than a pitch to the green from a well-placed tee shot. But mounds and traps embrace a green which is tilted towards you. The fifth hole (360 yd. par 4) is similar. Again the drive originates from a narrow chute, this time only 30 yards wide. You can hit it longer than at number 2 but the fairway is crowned, out of bounds borders the right, and deep stuff covers the embankment left. The largest tree prevents you from viewing the green even with a big hit, and again mounds and traps protect the putting surface.

At 436 yards, the par-5 eighth should yield more pars than it does. But unless you know the course well you'll lay up with your second shot, leaving a touchy third. A hillside that juts into the fairway right forces you to look left where a pond waits to draw you in. The finale is a par 3 behind the clubhouse. The pond that affected number 8 now must be negotiated in its entirety on this 135-yard test. With a trap behind the green, and water lapping up on the deep grass in front, Fox Run has saved the most precise tee shot for last. If you've successfully disposed of the water, a slippery contoured green where three putts are common could be the final insult.

Although the holes mentioned here supply quite a bit of trouble, the other five holes offer direct and forgiving paths to medium-sized, generally flat greens. Designed by Francis Duane (a partner of Robert Trent Jones), the course has matured well since 1969. A rerouting in the last five years has eliminated what was one of the most elevated tees in the state (the fifth hole, formerly the first). A final word of advice: Although we did not see any rats around Rat Pond (second hole) we suspect this is the breeding ground for numerous large, hungry, lonesome mosquitos. Come prepared.

HAYSTACK G.C.   Wilmington

Established: 1972 (opened 1985)

Number of Holes: 18

Yardages: Back, 6516; Middle, 6164; Forward, 5480

Par: 72, 74

Slope: 125, 120, 116

Fees: $26.00 ($15.00 for 9 holes) any day; gas carts must be rented weekends until 10:00 A.M.

Approximate Season: mid-May to mid-October

150-yard markers: White stakes on left

Carts: Motorized and pull

Starting Times: Recommended

Amenities: Full food and bar service

Telephone: 464–8301

Directions: Go north on Route 100 out of Wilmington about two miles. Take a left onto Cold Brook Road; follow signs over hill and through condos.

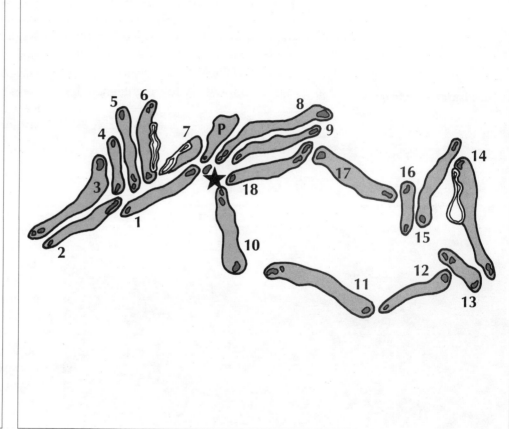

Designed almost twenty years ago by Desmond Muirhead, Haystack opened nine holes for play in 1973, and then corporate disaster struck. In 1984, the herculean work of restoring the completely overgrown course began with chainsaws. A full eighteen holes opened for play in 1986, and the grounds crew has continued to make refinements since then. Haystack has made great strides and will now compete with any course in Vermont for playability and challenge. Rolling fairways lined with trees appear to narrow then bend around and back in zigzag fashion yielding preferred landing areas on the short par 4s. The four par 3s are of a similar medium length (150–170 yards) and the longest par 5 can boast only 515 yards. Yet Haystack plays along hilly terrain displaying all the best qualities of Vermont mountain golf.

The fourth, an uphill 170-yard par 3, looks straightforward until you find yourself putting on the strongly sloped bilevel green. The 340-yard, par-4 fifth's green area is even more unusual in that a water bunker guards the right side. It's a mini-pond that has all the contours of a sand trap except it's wet. If this doesn't bother you, then both number 6 (300 yd. par 4) and number 7 (170 yd. par 3) will give you all the water you need. Both holes

Looking back on the tough fourteenth hole.

It's a long way down to the fairway from the elevated tee on 11.

green that features a rock wall and trap just behind, as well as traps front, center, and right.

The eleventh hole (500 yd. par 5) is way up there in the elevation contest. A perched tee overlooks a fairway that drops off around to the right (see photo). Without the two small traps left, you'd wonder where to hit. A good tee shot will carry a long way downhill, tempting you to hit your second shot onto a medium-sized green that is nearly surrounded by bunkers. But if you bounce off the back you'll be over mounds and down a steep embankment. Number 14 (515 yd. par 5) is notable for its length and hidden challenge. The tee shot is played over a mounded rise to an opening in the tree-lined fairway. From there you'll see the two hundred-plus yards of water hazard on the left that extends ahead all the way up to the green. Traps guard the front-center, right, and rear of this small raised green. Par here is hard won.

feature water on the left along most of the fairway. Number 8 (500 yd. par 5) has a large twin-trunked white birch squarely in the middle of your driving zone. The fairway then rolls and bends its way around and up to a well-guarded

107

Virtually every hole at Haystack has scenic vistas, including some outstanding "calendar shots." When we were there, the ball sat up well in the fairways composed of chewing fescue, colonial bentgrass, and perennial ryegrass in spite of damp conditions. The greens were in great shape considering their recent restoration; those on the back side had a different feel, as if more sand was used in the construction. Given good care, southern Vermont will have another championship-quality course. (Note: Haystack now requires appropriate attire, with guidelines similar to those at Woodstock.)

LAKE ST. CATHERINE C.C. Poultney

Established: 1925

Number of Holes: 9

Yardages: Middle, 6046; Forward, 5336

Par: 71, 72

Slope: 119, 112

Fees: $12.00 weekdays, $15.00 weekends ($10.00 after 4:00 P.M. any day)

Approximate Season: May 15 to October 15

150-yards markers: White disc in fairway

Carts: Motorized and pull

Starting Times: Available weekends

Amenities: Full food and bar service

Telephone: 287–9341

Directions: On the east side of Route 30, four miles south of Poultney.

This is a challenging course, being longer and more difficult than most of the nine-hole layouts in the state. In fact, from the red tees this is the longest course in Vermont. Its only drawback is a couple of congested spots, particularly where the first, fifth, and eighth greens converge. On the other hand its hilly terrain and numerous ditches makes it difficult to score well, and you may just need every club in your bag during a round—a refreshing change from drive and pitch.

The first hole is a 400-yard par 4 with a difficult second shot running downhill to a small green (keep it left if you hope to run it on the carpet). The third (160 yd. par 3) plays from a well-elevated tee to an even higher perched green. With a deep chasm between the two, traps flanking the green both left and right, and woods behind, this is no easy 3. The fourth is the toughest test on the course: a 414-yard par 4 from a narrow elevated tee with plenty of trouble on the right. This is where you may need that long iron, or more. The sixth and seventh are adjacent par 5s filled with sidehill lies and littered with sand traps. Both measure 510 yards but 6 plays uphill and 7 back down to the lowest area of the course. Watch out for the two traps in the middle of the fairway on 7. The eighth is a fairly short par 3 (160 yards) but if your shot leaks to the right you'll find one of those ditches, and if you pull it to the left you'll find it tough to take a full backswing in the cornfield (aren't Vermont courses wonderful?).

At first glance Lake St. Catherine seems like a straightforward layout. However, experience shows that it's trickier than it appears and requires your utmost concentration. Organized in 1925, the course has fully matured amongst the tall pine trees. Nearby Lake St. Catherine and the state park provide summer recreation for the entire family as well.

MANCHESTER C.C.

Established: 1969

Number of Holes: 18

Yardages: Back, 6724; Middle, 6164; Forward, 5408

Par: 72, 73

Slope: 127, 124, 116

Fees: $25.00 any time (mandatory cart rentals at all times)

Approximate Season: May 1 to October 25

150-yard markers: Bird houses on right

Carts: Motorized and pull

Starting Times: Recommended

Amenities: Full food and bar service

Telephone: 362–3148

Directions: On the east side of Route 7, a couple of miles north of Manchester Center.

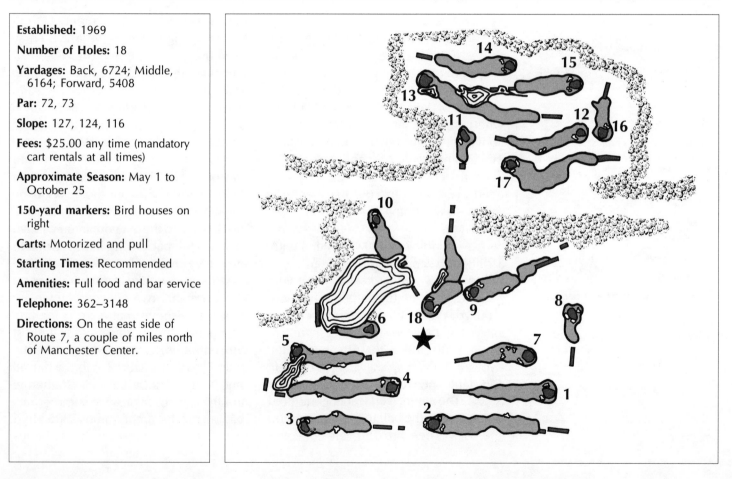

Manchester C.C. is a private club that may be played by staying at one of seventeen local lodging establishments, entering one of their two yearly charity tournaments, or with the Vermont Lung Association Golf Card. It's well worth the effort as this is one of the finest layouts in the state. Designed by Geoffrey Cornish and opened in 1969, the course features a back area of seven magnificent holes (11–17) framed by old maples and oaks. Unlike the first few holes, which play along Route 7, there are no distractions from the challenging golf at hand back here.

Your first critical placement shot comes on number 5, a dogleg 371-yard par 4. The best drive finds the left half of the fairway just inside the traps. There's no room for error with the approach. A pond fronts 90 percent of this large green and traps border the sides. The entire surface is contoured and it rejects the ball to the front and off the back. There are 150 yards of water to carry on the 207-yard, par-3 sixth. The green is slanted towards the tee with flanking rear mounds and traps, plus a fifteen-foot drop-off behind everything. Stay below the flagstick (but above the water). All of this has been but a warm up for the back side, which starts with a drive over water on number 10 (339 yd. par 4). When you leave the green, cross the railroad tracks, and curl around to the eleventh tee, you've found some of the best golf in New England. The long slim green on this 146-yard par 3 is above the tee, and angles away from you out of sight. Majestic maple trees frame the carpet. Number 12 is about as narrow as 369-yard par 4s come. Consider an iron from the tee as a fairway trap leaves little bail out area in the driving zone. The hole concludes at the only double green in Vermont, which is connected to the sixteenth's by a narrow peninsula with a white birch tree growing from it. Though all the holes have had rugged terrain, number 13 (531 yd. par 5) has the most so far. It bends, pitches, and rolls around two ponds on

The sixth plays back towards the clubhouse over 150 yards of water.

its way to an elevated green that few players will hit in two. On the other hand, the seventeenth is the kind of par 5 that will tempt even the average player, and it will yield an occasional eagle. The largest oak of all, directly in the middle of the sloped fairway, forces you to flirt with deep woods to its left, or accept a more circuitous route around to the right. With this hazard safely negotiated, your shot into the small green is complicated only by three surrounding traps.

Everything about the greens at Manchester is right. They're medium to large sized, subtly modulated and sloped, firm but not sandy, fair and a bit on the quick side. Not all the fairways are narrow, but none is broad. Light rough is consistent and you can play from many wooded areas. The sand is deep and uniform. Water influences seven holes and rolling hillsides most of the rest. Of the many fine courses by Mr. Cornish in Vermont, this is the best!

MT. ANTHONY C.C.

Established: 1897

Number of Holes: 18

Yardages: Back, 6206; Middle, 5941; Forward, 4941

Par: 71, 72

Slope: 127, 125, 109

Fees: $10.00 for 9 holes, $18.00 for 18 holes ($7.00 for 9 holes and $10.00 for 18 holes after 4:30 P.M.) any day

Approximate Season: April to October

150-yard markers: Flower pots on right

Carts: Motorized and pull

Starting Times: Required weekends, available weekdays

Amenities: Full food and bar service

Telephone: 447–7079

Directions: From downtown Bennington take Main St. west to Convent Ave. Go north one mile; course is on left.

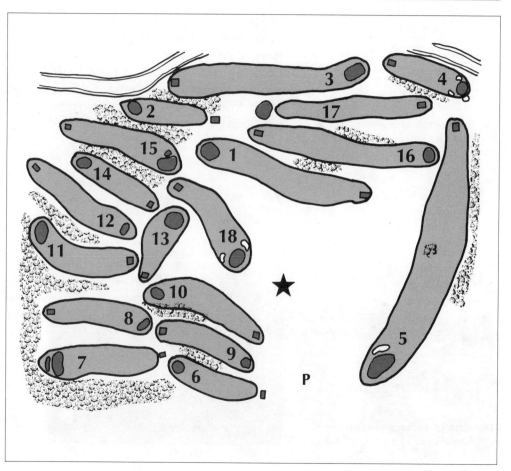

113

The southwest corner of the state occupies a special niche in the history of golf in Vermont. The private Ekwanok C.C. and Dorset Field Club, and the public Mt. Anthony are all pre-1900. In fact, the September 9, 1899, edition of the Boston Herald is headlined "Golf Played on Mountains in Vermont." It goes on to describe the new layout at Mt. Anthony, the site of which had previously been the cow pastures of two local farmers. The view of downtown Bennington has changed a bit over the years, but the mountains in the distance, the Bennington Monument in the background, and the terrain out on the course have stayed about the same—it's still golf on mountains.

From the elevated first tee it's easy to fade your ball into an unseen creek bordering the fairway. And you'll have to be much more precise from the second tee (182 yd. par 3) as large willow trees line both sides of the fairway and narrow to the green. This time the Walloomsac River waits unseen to snag the slice. It also haunts the fourth (104 yd. par 3), where a row of pines frames the opposite side of the hole and three traps embrace the green. The sixth begins a string of eight holes of true mountain golf. Although none of them are over 379 yards you'll find flat lies few

The Bennington Monument towers over the Mt. Anthony fairways.

114

and far between, the greens small, fast, and undulating, steep embankments common, and a blind shot or two to boot. There's all that and more on number 7 (338 yd. par 4). Here your best drive will barely let you see the top of the flag. The green on the uphill 379-yard, par-4 tenth may be the toughest on the course. Your shot to it is blind, trees line the left side, and it's a steep and slippery sidehill surface with no easy pin placements. The teeing ground on the 156-yard, par-3 thirteenth towers sixty-five feet above the green, but it is flat down there and par is possible. Back into the willows on the 304-yard, par-4 fifteenth. A ditch angles through the fairway here but at least you're back on the level part of the layout.

The clubhouse at Mt. Anthony is a large, comfortable facility with the "best food in Bennington" according to its friendly staff. An international-style menu is served up daily for lunch and dinner. The public may also enjoy a driving range, paddle and regular tennis courts, and an eighteen-by thirty-two-foot swimming pool. The course itself displays the much smaller old-style greens, lovely mountain views, and the historic monument as a backdrop. And roughly ninety years after its debut, Mt. Anthony remains a prime example of golf on mountains in Vermont.

MT. SNOW C.C.

Dover

Established: 1970

Number of Holes: 18

Yardages: Back, 6894; Middle, 6443; Forward, 5839

Par: 72, 74

Slope: 130, 127, 120

Fees: $27.00 ($13.00 after 4:30 P.M.) any day

Approximate Season: mid-May to mid-October

150-yard markers: Red posts

Carts: Motorized and pull

Starting Times: Required

Amenities: Full food and bar service

Note: The course is closed to the public at some times in season due to golf school.

Telephone: 464–3333

Directions: Heading south on Route 100 into West Dover, watch for sign and access road on right.

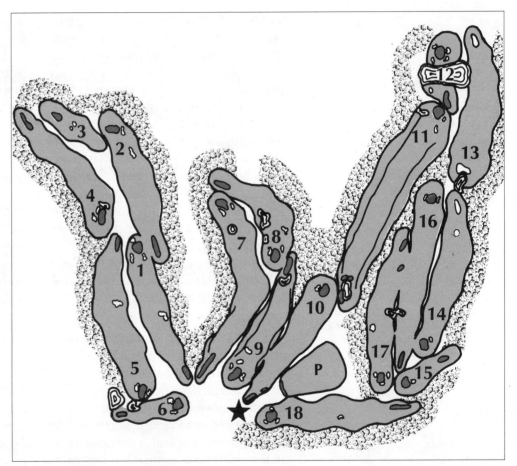

The Mount Snow region has nearly everything to offer as a four-season destination resort. Not only is there a beautifully maintained championship eighteen-hole Geoffrey Cornish course, but a nationally recognized golf school operates all season. Because of this you'll need to schedule your arrival at the course as noted above. At times the clubhouse and numerous practice areas can be busy. With rolling to hilly terrain, this layout has forty-three traps of fine, consistent sand and a substantial number of water hazards. Though definitely in the mountain golf category, Mt. Snow is more gentle and less precipitous than many such courses and therefore easier to score on as well.

The 344-yard, par-4 fourth's relatively short length gives you a thoughtful option: lay up for a good, level lie or go for it all to catch the downhill slope and get maximum rolling distance. If you cut the slight corner too much, you may still be able to find your ball in the open trees on the right. Your approach is the main challenge, as two large traps guard the green center and right front, and a pond the left side. The terrain rolls back up toward the right to create two levels with a substantial mid-slope on the large green.

532-yard number 7 is not the longest par 5 but is rated the number 1 handicap hole. Your take-off from the elevated tee is somewhat narrow but the fairway widens out and spills off to the right as you reach the lower and more level area at the dogleg. You'll need a big hit out to center-right to hit your second at the green. Since the shot will be off a sidehill lie, play it safe and stay short of the pond on the left and wet area on the right. You'll find yourself on relatively level ground with a well-lofted iron shot needed to clear the pair of front traps.

Number 11 (577 yd. par 5) has the distinction of being the second longest par 5 in Vermont. Though fairly level, it is narrow, water hazards line either side, and deep roughs border all the way to the green. There the trees are thick and

Downhill lies are the rule on number 4.

nasty. A small pond left-front and two traps—one green-side, the other front right—ice the cake. The 147-yard, par-3 twelfth is all carry across a large pond to the biggest green in the state. Four large traps of various shapes guard each corner. The same pond runs along the right side of 403-yard, par-4 number 13 early on but this is not the water to worry about. What you won't see on your long shot into the narrow, boomerang-shaped green is a pond immediately off the back set into the interior bend. Holes 16 and 17 share another pond, all but hidden from either tee. The pond waits for any shot left of center and is particularly troublesome for 17.

Nine new holes are scheduled to open in 1990. Current holes 7, 8, and 9 will be combined with six new holes to create a course for the exclusive use of the golf school. New holes to replace the old 7, 8, and 9 will be added to the existing course.

Mt. Snow's fairways are for the most part wide open, rolling, and lined with trees far enough apart to enable a good recovery shot out of playable light rough. Water and sand are very much in the picture; both hazards are designed to make you stop and consider nearly every shot towards the green. Large, pitched putting surfaces feature tightly knit turf and true readings. In 1984 Mt. Snow hosted the New England PGA Championship. For more information about the golf school write to The Golf School, Mt. Snow, Vermont, 05356 or call for reservations (1-800-451-4211 from the northeast including Ohio, Virginia and West Virginia).

STAMFORD VALLEY GOLF COURSE Stamford

Established: late 1950s

Number of Holes: 9

Yardages: Back, 5900; Middle, 5430; Forward, 4694

Par: 72

Fees: $3.50 per 9 holes weekdays, $4.00 weekends

Approximate Season: May through October

150-yard markers: None

Carts: Motorized and pull

Starting Times: Required Sunday mornings, otherwise not necessary

Amenities: Light food and beer

Telephone: 694–9144

Directions: Take a left off Routes 8 and 100 south just past the stone lions in Stamford onto Lane Road. Clubhouse is a quarter mile down the road on the right.

If you're heading south and miss the turn to Stamford Valley you'll be in Massachusetts in seconds. But turn around, because the least-expensive nine-hole course in the state is definitely worth the visit. You'll wonder why as you pull into the parking lot and gaze out over a flat, featureless field that contains the first three holes. But believe us, things get better quickly. And you've got to admit: the views to the southernmost of Vermont's Green Mountains are spectacular.

At 392 yards from the white tees, number 4 is the shortest real par 5 we've ever seen. A fine long drive will leave you in a lower fairway area aiming at a 35- by 50-yard landing zone 150 to 200 yards away. You must lay up from here as you're prevented from going for the green by a line of trees that constitutes a second dogleg on this hole. With some back-to-front pitch to the green itself, and deep unplayable stuff to the right, this hole probably produces fewer birdies than many straight 500-yard par 5s. The sixth (326 yd. par 4) is another example of a short hole that will frustrate good golfers into sixes and sevens. You must drive uphill to a very small prime landing zone defined by a gap in a row of trees (aim at the end of the pines and before the apples). From here the uphill, side-sloping fairway angles off at forty-five degrees to a large but unseen putting surface set in a side slope. The seventh is a tough 215-yard par 3. From an elevated tee at the edge of the woods you hit down across a large gully with a tall pine growing from it. It's all carry up to this large green with a drop-off behind it. Played from the blue tees (which does add an extra dimension everywhere on this layout), number 8 (355 yd. par 4) is stretched to 400 yards with a drive over water. From there it's uphill to another unseen green. However, this one is more contoured than the other eight and rolls off sharply front and left.

As far from country club or resort golf as you can get, Stamford Valley is still really fine public golf. The fairways are a mixture of field grasses, but the greens are generally uniform and quick despite being shaggy in places. There's not a sand trap to be seen and only one (sneaky) pond 240 yards out on number 5. But there's plenty of challenge and lots of fun for the money. For laid-back golf, it's worth a stop when you're down that way.

STRATTON MOUNTAIN C.C.

Established: 1965 (Lake and Mountain), 1986 (Forest)

Number of Holes: 27

Yardages: Lake: Back, 3325; Middle, 3066; Forward, 2700

Mountain: Back, 3277; Middle, 3041; Forward, 2710

Forest: Back, 3201; Middle, 2978; Forward, 2453

Par: 36, 37 for each nine

Slope: Lake-Forest: 125, 122, 113; Forest-Mountain: 126, 123, 113

Fees: $35.00 for 18 holes, $20.00 for 9 holes any day

Approximate Season: May 1 to October 20

150-yard markers: Brown stakes on right

Carts: Motorized and pull

Starting Times: Required 24-hours in advance

Amenities: Full food and bar service

Telephone: 297–1880

Directions: Take Stratton Mountain access road from Route 30 in Bondville.

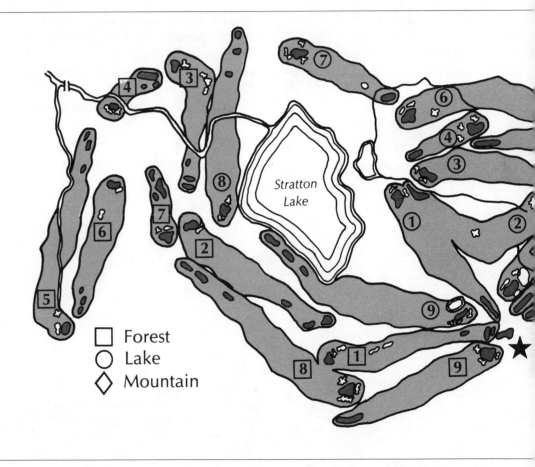

Stratton Lake

☐ Forest
◯ Lake
◇ Mountain

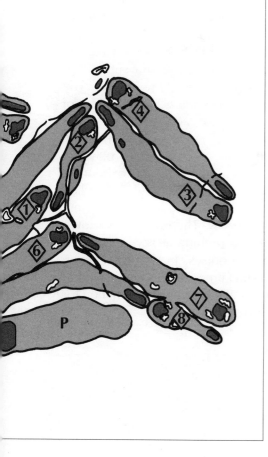

Besides twenty-seven holes of Geoffrey Cornish-designed golf, Stratton Mountain Resort also features a twenty-two-acre training site for its golf school. Better yet, the courses are now open to the public—they had been open only to Stratton residents and golf school participants—with a call to set up a tee time a day in advance. The layout features three separate nines. Lake and Mountain have been in operation since 1965 with the Forest nine added twenty years later and opened for play on July 1, 1986.

On the Lake leg, number 2 is a sharp left-hand dogleg (395 yd. par 4). A star-shaped trap is hidden in the corner and a sprawling four-lobed sand bunker protects the plateaued green front and left. The seventh (193 yd. par 3) requires a full shot up a rise to a medium-sized green above the tee. Your shot must carry a ditch early on, then avoid sand left and a grass bunker set in the hillside right. The drive on number 8 (390 yd. par 4) is downhill but must carry another ditch. This one is 150 yards out and lined with tall reeds, small trees, and large rocks. The green is set in a grove of trees with the lake close by to the left and sand on the corners. Number 9 (508 yd. par 5) makes the most use of Stratton Lake, which these three holes have framed. From the white tees one must carry 180 yards of water to a narrow landing zone framed by trees with no bail-out area. From there the hole heads uphill past a boulder in fairway right to a long narrow green with sand to the right and more water on the left.

The Mountain nine features the longest hole in Vermont—a 621-yard monster from the blue. This hole, the fifth, is characteristically Stratton with ditches everywhere. One borders the first 300 yards of the fairway right, and two cross your path from there on in. The tee and green are both slightly elevated and trees (from which one can play out of) border the left-hand side. The green plays faster than most and is embraced by the normal complement of three traps. Seemingly innocent number 7 (358 yd. par 4)

123

Even the Lake Nine has substantial terrain and deep woods.

is not what it appears. The prime landing zone is pinched to a scant ten yards wide by a fairway trap right and a small pond out of sight left. Hit it really big and straight or be smart and lay up.

This is nearly perfect resort golf. The putting surfaces are generally large, of medium speed, and without severe undulations. The fairways are not narrow and may be bordered by playable wooded areas rather than out of bounds. The sand, though plentiful, is predictable and, like all the hazards, in view on most holes. There is up-and-down terrain, but nothing as severe as other mountain courses. In short, challenge exists with fairness in this scenic natural setting. Stratton is a great destination for your next golf vacation.

Established: 1967

Number of Holes: 9

Yardages: Back, 6694; Middle, 6454; Forward, 5488

Par: 72, 74

Slope: 126, 124, 117

Fees: $12.00 weekdays, $17.00 weekends ($7.00 after 5:00 P.M. any day)

Note: League play after 5:00 P.M. on Tuesday, Wednesday, and Friday has priority

Approximate Season: May 1 to October 31

150-yard markers: Marks on trees

Carts: Motorized and pull

Starting Times: Required weekends

Amenities: Full food and bar service

Telephone: 875–2517

Directions: Take Route 11 about four miles east from Londonderry to Popple Dungeon Road. Take right to clubhouse.

Tater Hill Resort is a complete recreational facility with a nine-hole golf course, tennis courts, swimming pool and deck, nature trails, cross-country skiing in winter, and a small landing strip. Tucked into a valley surrounded by mountains, the view from much of the course reveals little sign of habitation—A fine spot for a golf getaway while the family enjoys the pool and facilities.

The layout begins with a 443-yard par 5. Your tee shot is to the unseen hilltop fairway where traps block the right-hand shortcut to the green. To reach it in two you'll have to carry two small ponds on the right and an embankment fronting the green. The picturesque third (168 yd. par 3) plays over another pond with a stone wall and trees on the left, and flanking front bunkers guarding the green. Numbers 2, 4, and 6 are parallel and traverse the top of a common hill. Each has a backboard behind the green to show direction for an otherwise blind shot. Number 7 (313 yd. par 4) takes a ninety-degree left-hand turn around an outcropping of trees at the edge of deep woods. The second shot is inclined up to an undulating putting surface with traps embracing the left and right front. Number 9 measures 601 yards from the blue tees, making it the third longest hole in the state. It's laid out over rolling sidehill terrain with a pond coming into play on the right and woods to the left. It finishes to an oblong green tucked into a hill below the pool.

Tater Hill is long (3202 yards) and has the highest course rating (70.3) of any nine-holer in Vermont. You'll need every club in your bag here and more. The "more" would start with insect repellant, as the course provides an ample supply of black flies when the breeze stops blowing across the south-facing hillside. The fairways are broad, the grass thick, and maintenance excellent. A large lounge is your stopover before it's on to tennis, swimming, or another nine holes.

Established: 1921

Number of Holes: 9

Yardages: Middle, 5382; Forward, 4924

Par: 68, 72

Slope: 103, 101

Fees: $12.00 weekdays, $18.00 weekends ($10.00 after 4:00 P.M. on weekends)

Approximate Season: May 1 to November 1

150-yard markers: Evergreen bushes with orange stakes

Carts: Motorized and pull

Starting Times: Recommended weekends

Amenities: Full food and bar service

Telephone: 674–6491

Directions: From Exit 9 of I-91, take Route 5 south about two miles. Course on left north of Windsor.

There's more to this course than a quick drive by would reveal. A retirement-aged summer crowd finds the course in good shape with well-cared for greens and sand superior to that of many other clubs in Vermont. Play takes place on three distinct levels, and except for an unfortunate crossover on the fifth and sixth, the course makes fine use of the terrain and limited area. Recently installed irrigation has eliminated fairway burnout, a problem in the past.

The first two holes and the drive on number 3 play along the main clubhouse level. Your second shot on the third (326 yd. par 4) is up a steep hill to an unseen green that rolls off to the front. It's all carry back to the pin or you could end up down on the fairway from whence you came. Number 7 (133 yd. par 3) plays from right in front of the clubhouse to a well-trapped putting surface on the lower level. That bunker in front is much bigger than it looks, so having enough club is vital. If you're over the green, it's possible to pitch clear back across it and still find the sand. The eighth (449 yd. par 5) is bordered by railroad tracks; a long exact second shot is needed to reach the small, narrow green. Don't risk being right, left, or long as deep rough starts immediately on those three sides.

A great porch on the folksy clubhouse is perfect for sipping inexpensive Buds (about the best price in the state), and the food prices are reasonable also. The avid senior membership, the proximity to the Upper Valley, and the easy access from Interstate 91 make for some crowded mornings at Windsor. We advise a call ahead. But wide-open fairways offer plenty of room for everyone's shots, so relax and enjoy the three par 3s, five par 4s, and one par 5 on this casual layout.

APPENDIXES

It was said in the late 1800s that anywhere the Scots emigrated, a golf club was soon to follow. Such was the case in Montreal, indisputably the birthplace of golf in North America. Records show there had been social clubs which took the name "golf" earlier in the southern United States, but none have survived into the twentieth century. There can be no doubt however, of Scotsmen chasing the gutty (from "gutta-percha") around a field on Logan's Farm in Montreal during the 1850's and 1860's, and the establishment of the first club and course in Fletcher's Field at Mount Royal Park on November 4, 1873. It is curious that the Royal Montreal Golf Club and its founder, Alexander Dennistoun, could not effect an interest in the sport a scant fifty miles away in Vermont, even though well-publicized yearly matches between Montreal and Quebec City raged from 1876 onward.

But once again it was the Scots who fired the first shots in Vermont. In the summer of 1886 a vacationing group from Troy, New York, and New York City found the fields around Dorset to their liking, laid out a nine-hole course, and established the Dorset Field Club. Although they have photos so dated as well as a list of founding members including first president A. W. Harrington, there is no dated written record or minutes of this historic event. If the date could be firmly substantiated, Dorset would take its place before the St. Andrews Club of Yonkers, New York, which is recognized as the country's oldest continually operating club, founded November 14, 1888. While the course site for St. Andrews was moved several years later, Dorset still golfs on part of the original layout.

British Open champion Willy Park, Jr., visited the United States for the first time in 1895. After a match at St. Andrew's in Yonkers, Park was invited to Dr. Seward Webb's estate, Shelburne Farms. A nine-hole 3010-yard, par-36 golf links was established on the banks of Lake Champlain, and the Webb family received instruction from Park for three days. The Doctor's wife, Lila, was the most avid student and played until near her death in 1936. The course saw use until World War II, when it fell victim to gas rationing.

In Manchester, George A. Orvis built a six-hole course on open land behind the Equinox House and the Hillside Golf Club was organized in 1895. One year later the course was extended to nine holes with the addition of land belonging to Judge Loveland Munson. A new clubhouse was built and in 1899 the name was changed to the Equinox Golf Club. Also in 1895 D. B. Harrington, a Boston physician, knocked his ball around a field in Woodstock and soon a course was established on Mt. Peg. It was moved twice before settling into its current home in 1906 when Scot William Tucker, Sr., laid out nine holes. Golf was played in three locations in Bennington by 1895: a few holes at Samuel Robinson's farm by the railroad underpass, a couple on James C. Colgate's place "Ben Venue," and a small private links at Frederic B. Jennings's "Fairview." Banding together to create a nine-hole course, the latter two men (among others) founded Mt. Anthony Country Club in 1897. The layout was built on the Griswold Farm but lasted only until 1905 when the club assumed the present location.

By the mid-1890s golf was also played in Rutland on links along Clement Road south of Otter Creek towards Center Rutland. The year 1897 found a membership of twenty-one and the first documented tournament in the state—a putting contest with forty-two entrants that took place on October 1, 1897. The club flourished here until the Baxter Farm was purchased in 1902. There George Low, Sr., laid out nine holes, five of which are still in use today. In 1898 Mrs. Jane MacKenzie introduced golf to summer residents of Greensboro. Three short holes were tried in a pasture by D. R. Stuart's cottage and then five set in a field east of the village after interest was aroused. As with many layouts of the era, tomato cans were sunk into less-rough portions of a field—greens were purely hypothetical. When the summer crew returned in 1899, a full nine-hole course was established on the current site and except for several modifications Mountain View Country Club remains today as one of Vermont's authentic nineteenth century golfing grounds.

There were other pockets of golf in the northern part of the state by 1899. Links were laid out in Hyde Park during that year and played until 1902 when the Moss Meadow Golf Club was formed and a course built at "Roddy Flats." This served until 1916 when the Lamoille County Country Club was organized and the construction of the nine-hole course on Gavin Tyndall's land was begun and followed by a clubhouse in 1921. Lamoille closed during the war years of the forties. Alex Findlay of Boston designed a nine-hole course on the Underclyffe property, a high pasture northwest of St. Johnsbury. Named for the largest tree on the summit of the hill, Old Pine Golf Club opened in September 1899. A clubhouse was built in 1902 and play continued until World War I.

Just south of Burlington on the east side of Route 7, the Waubanakee Golf Club opened its sporty nine-hole course in 1899 as well. This 3115-yard par 36 hosted the Vermont Amateur in 1903, 1914, 1917, and 1922. In 1924 a splinter group formed Burlington Country Club, but Waubanakee continued until the 1940s. On September 18, 1902, the Montpelier Country Club formally opened its clubhouse and grounds on the former Sam Smith farm. The golf course was ready for play the next year and is now operated by the Elks at the same location.

Back down south, golf had spread beyond Manchester, Bennington, and Dorset. In 1899 the Wantastiquet Golf Club was established in Brattleboro and a six-hole layout was played around the ski-jump hillside. A bungalow served as clubhouse until the club, renamed the Brattleboro Country Club, moved to its present location in 1914. Also in 1899, the Ondawa Club was formed in Arlington and a nine-hole course took shape on church-owned land south of town in the Lost Lake area. But in just a few years it was gone.

By 1898 James L. Taylor and other big-city summer residents of Manchester saw the need for a first-rate championship eighteen-hole course in the area. They liked the Schuyler Farm on the southeast side of the village and invited Walter Travis and John Duncan Dunn to inspect it. The land was purchased in August 1899 and a crew of fifty began work early in the fall. The course was opened in June 1900 with twelve holes in play, and by mid-July all eighteen were completed. Ekwanok Country Club ushered in a new era in Vermont golf. Today this very private course retains the same routing as in 1900, with some modification to eight holes by Geoffrey Cornish being the only remodeling. One of the finest courses in the country in the early 1900s, it hosted the 1914 U.S. Amateur.

Although ongoing regional matches were established immediately, a statewide organization was needed to oversee match play. In 1902 representatives met and formed the Vermont Golf Association. Charter members Montpelier, Old Pine, Waubanakee, Mt. Anthony, Dorset, and Rutland were joined by Barre and Ekwanok the next year. Today the V.G.A. lists fifty member clubs and runs twenty-five yearly events.

By 1925 there were thirty courses in Vermont. The sport flourished during this, the golden age of golf, but the depression of the thirties and the war years of the forties took a heavy toll. By the time the era of the resort course began in the fifties, many clubs had disappeared. The Midway Golf Club, a privately owned course in Barre, and the Bristol Country Club, a natural layout designed by George Frazer, are two examples. Kingsbery Farms Hotel had a course in Derby under the supervision of Ralph Barton, co-builder of courses at Yale, Dartmouth, and Mid-Ocean in Bermuda. The Hampton Golf Course in Fair Haven was less than a quarter mile from the New York border, and on the opposite side of the state Wells-Wood Golf Club was a stone's throw from New Hampshire. Northern golfing enclaves were once served by the Hardwick Country Club and the Lyndon Golf Club. National Life Insurance had a course for employees and others just a five-minute walk from downtown Montpelier. In the south we've lost another Ralph Barton design at Wilmington, and the only William Flynn layout in Hartwellville.

The expansion of golf in the last thirty years has come mostly under the direction of the resorts. It began at Stowe in 1956 and continued down the backbone of mountains that divide the state and provide the East Coast's best skiing. Sugarbush built a course in 1964, Stratton in 1965, Manchester in 1969, Mt. Snow in 1970, and Quechee in 1970 and 1975. Although there were also closings during this time (Quarry Hill of Burlington and Barton Country Club in the sixties, Hyde Manor in Sudbury in the seventies, and Bonnie Oaks in Fairlee in the eighties) the course list has grown from thirty-nine in 1964 to fifty-seven in 1988.

During the early 1980s eighteen-hole courses were opened slopeside at Killington and in the shadow of Mt. Mansfield at West Bolton. Champlain Country Club and Stratton Mountain each added nine holes to their

131

existing layouts. Farm Resort in the Stowe area was rescued from near extinction and reopened in 1985. A course planned by Desmond Muirhead (and actually started ten years ago) opened for play in 1985 at Haystack.

Growth in the second half of this decade has been slower. Wolf Run in Bakersfield opened nine holes in 1987 and plans to continue building when its downhill ski area is under way. Essex Country Club established nine holes in 1988 and another nine are currently under construction. The Geoffrey Cornish-designed Bonny Braes is a second course also under construction in Essex. Last, Proctor-Pittsford is the only nine-hole club to have added an additional loop in the 1980s.

Vermont has seen few new courses successfully negotiate the Act 250 approval process. Three courses are currently in various stages of this elaborate ritual. Ascutney Mountain has asked Robert Trent Jones, Jr., for a second plan that would have less environmental impact than his first proposal. It is hoped that construction will start in the spring of 1989. Straddling the Stratton/Jamaica town line is the Tamarack Project,

an eighteen-hole championship course designed by Arnold Palmer. With an absence of zoning in Jamaica and a pro-development attitude in Stratton, it was thought that Tamarack would gain quick approval in the summer of 1988. Such was not the case, and as of the winter of 1989 no decisions had been reached.

Paul Truax has been trying to build a Charles Ankrom—Raymond Floyd design at Sherman Hollow in Huntington for the past four years. Despite an innovative Integrated Pest Management program to control the use of pesticides, repeated meetings with the Vermont Department of Health and the EPA, and endorsement by the Green Mountain Audubon Conservation Committee, Sherman Hollow was denied its Act 250 permit in 1988. With strong local support, the club filed for reconsideration in November 1988.

Two other clubs in Windham County (Sage Hill and Sunbowl) are about to open the door to the Act 250 tunnel, and Montague in Randolph seeks approval to double in size from nine to eighteen holes. Let's hope some of these new golfing holes are built to help satisfy the increasing demand for more golf in the 1990s.

APPENDIX B   Course Ratings and Slope for All V.G.A. Clubs

This is the latest (August 1988) list of course data for Vermont Golf Association members. In order to arrive at slope figures, remeasuring and rerating took place during the latter part of 1986. Subsequent editions of this book will incorporate new data as it becomes available.

What is the new Slope System all about? The U.S.G.A. decided that the old handicapping system was not fair enough, that it did not take into account local factors for players of all levels. (The course rating, which is used to adjust handicaps for local conditions, really reflects difficulty for only the best players.) The Slope System should help to quantify the many variables that contribute to each course's degree of difficulty. It will therefore allow any golfer anywhere to travel to another course and play others on even terms. Exactly how this is done is beyond the scope of this book; consult your club pro for further information.

	Holes	Back Tees	Course Rating	Slope	Middle Tees	Course Rating	Slope	Forward Tees	Course Rating	Slope
Alburg	18	————	69.4	110	6287	68.7	109	5747	65.7	97
Barre	18	6191	70.2	123	5986	69.2	119	5515	67.1	116
Basin Harbor	18	6513	71.5	122	6232	70.4	120	5805	68.1	116
Bellows Falls	9	————	68.2	114	5807	67.0	109	5292	64.6	106
Blush Hill	9	————	63.0	101	4730	62.6	100	4534	61.6	96
Bomoseen	9	————	66.0	114	5010	64.0	107	4420	61.6	101
Bradford	9	————	60.6	102	4154	60.6	102	4024	60.0	101
Brattleboro	9	————	71.8	121	5950	69.8	117	5815	67.7	108
Burlington	18	6514	71.7	124	6356	71.0	123	5699	68.0	116
Champlain	18	6145	69.9	120	5976	68.9	119	5217	66.0	112
Copley	9	————	66.0	105	5550	65.4	104	5020	63.6	98

	Holes	Back Tees	Course Rating	Slope	Middle Tees	Course Rating	Slope	Forward Tees	Course Rating	Slope
Crown Point	18	6572	72.0	123	6120	70.0	119	5542	67.2	114
Dorset	9	2973	68.4	124	2788	67.4	117	2551	65.2	110
Ekwanok	18	6545	71.4	122	6145	69.6	120	5916	68.4	118
Enosburg Falls	9	5680	67.6	114	5568	66.8	113	5284	65.6	109
Equinox	18	6451	71.1	123	6022	68.9	119	5278	65.1	112
Essex	9	6498	71.6	121	6350	70.4	121	5414	65.8	111
Farm Resort	9	6038	68.8	111	5798	67.6	108	5198	65.0	106
Fox Run	9	———	67.2	108	5280	65.6	106	5094	64.2	102
Haystack	18	6516	71.5	125	6164	69.8	120	5480	66.8	116
Killington	18	6326	71.3	134	5896	70.2	132	5664	69.0	128
Kwiniaska	18	7067	72.7	125	6796	71.4	122	5911	68.1	117
Lake Morey	18	5869	67.9	110	5605	66.7	108	5117	64.2	101
Lake St. Catherine	9	———	69.8	120	6046	68.8	119	5336	66.2	112
Manchester	18	6724	71.9	127	6164	69.3	124	5408	66.1	116
Marble Island	9	5228	66.2	111	5086	65.6	110	4436	62.6	103
Ralph Myhre-Middlebury	18	6379	71.3	129	6014	69.6	126	5309	66.6	120
Montague	9	———	67.6	116	5780	67.0	116	5368	65.8	112
Montpelier	9	5326	66.6	114	5158	65.9	113	4920	64.9	110
Mt. Anthony	18	6206	70.5	127	5941	69.2	125	4941	63.3	109
Mt. Snow	18	6894	73.3	130	6443	71.1	127	5839	68.1	120
Mountain View	9	———	67.6	112	5538	66.6	110	4878	64.0	105

SOURCE: Vermont Golf Association

	Holes	Back Tees	Course Rating	Slope	Middle Tees	Course Rating	Slope	Forward Tees	Course Rating	Slope
Neshobe	9	——	67.8	120	5575	66.8	120	5191	64.8	117
Newport	18	——	70.3	120	6219	69.2	117	5544	66.0	110
Northfield	9	5902	69.3	119	5728	68.8	115	4828	64.7	109
Orleans	18	6123	69.3	117	5934	68.5	115	5545	66.7	111
Proctor-Pittsford	9	——	67.7	125	5721	67.5	125	5530	66.6	123
Quechee (Highland)	18	6765	73.1	129	6341	70.4	123	5439	67.2	119
Quechee (Lakeland)	18	6103	70.3	128	5627	68.4	124	5061	65.8	117
Richford	9	——	68.6	116	6002	68.2	113	5700	67.2	112
Rocky Ridge	18	——	69.7	122	5938	68.8	120	5236	65.6	114
Rutland	18	6062	70.4	129	5761	69.0	127	5368	65.9	121
St. Johnsbury	9	——	70.2	115	6064	69.2	114	5786	65.2	103
Stowe	18	6156	70.2	122	5772	68.4	121	5346	66.6	115
Stratton (Lake-Forest)	18	6650	71.2	125	6132	69.4	122	5400	65.0	113
Stratton (Forest-Mountain)	18	6554	71.2	126	6082	69.3	123	5420	65.2	113
Sugarbush	18	6524	71.7	128	5886	69.0	122	5187	66.1	114
Tater Hill	9	6694	73.0	126	6454	71.4	124	5488	67.0	117
West Bolton	18	——	66.3	109	5432	65.6	109	5074	62.4	103
White River*	9	——	——	——	5600	64.0	100	5226	62.0	98
Windsor	9	——	66.2	105	5382	65.0	103	4924	63.6	101
Williston	18	5504	67.4	118	5206	65.8	113	4738	63.2	106
Wolf Run		——	——	——	5940	69.0	115	5220	——	——
Woodstock	18	6001	69.2	121	5555	67.3	117	4956	64.1	109

Besides the golf clubs mentioned in this book, there are other courses to play as well as places just to hit balls. These range from pitching courses around many a country farm to several totally private clubs. The following listing is the result of our research. If we've missed you, take it as an indication that you might not be doing enough publicity, and accept our apologies.

PAR-3 COURSES

Sitzmark: This course is part of the Sitzmark Resort facility just off Route 100 in Wilmington and includes a pool, tennis, and lodging. Here in a couple of large open fields is an eighteen-hole, par-3 course measuring 1982 yards. Holes range from 90 to 155 yards and play to small and medium-sized greens, twice across water. 464–3384.

Apple Tree Bay: This campground and marina also have a very casual nine-hole, par-3 layout. On Route 2 in South Hero. 372–5398.

Wilcox Cove: This is not a par-3 course, yet the longest hole is only a 250-yard par 4. The nine holes stretch out over 1705 yards of very gently rolling property just a line of trees away from Lake Champlain in Grand Isle. Originally a boys' camp with a six-hole course, Wilcox Cove is free to occupants of the cabins for rent here, and may be played by the public for a $5.00 fee weekdays and $6.00 Sundays. A charming place to learn the game, the club is open from May to October 30 but is often crowded in July and August. Call 372–8343 for further details.

PRIVATE COURSES

Ekwanok Country Club: Designed by Walter Travis and John Duncan Dunn and opened in June 1900, this course remains today as one of New England's finest. It is Vermont's only club to have hosted a major golf event: the 1914 U.S. Amateur, where Francis Ouimet beat Jerry Travers 6 and 5. It is totally private and play is as a guest of a member only.

Dorset Field Club: Until 1984 a member of the public could play at Dorset by staying at the Barrows House or other approved accomodations in Dorset. This is no longer the case, as play is now restricted to the four hundred members and their guests. The nine-hole layout has evolved from golfing grounds originally laid out in 1886, one of America's first courses.

A.D. Dana Estate: Mr. Arthur D. Dana, Jr., of New York City and Stowe, Vermont, has maintained a nine-hole, 3400-yard layout on his former dairy farm at Stowe since 1967. Designed by Canadian architect Howard Watson, the course is for the use of Mr. Dana, his family, and invited guests only.

SEMI-PRIVATE COURSES

The following courses appear in our regular entries, but limit play by the public in the following manner.

Quechee: As a Quechee landowner or tenant, as a player in the New England Open, or with the Vermont Lung Association Golf Card.

Manchester: In one of two yearly benefit tournaments, by staying in one of seventeen local lodges, or with the Vermont Lung Card.

Brattleboro: Must be from outside of the local area, and then only Monday through Thursday, or Friday mornings before 11:30 A.M.

Burlington: The public may play after 2:00 P.M. prior to Memorial Day or after Labor Day.

GOLF COURSES CLOSE TO VERMONT

Though golf in Vermont is unique, there are similar experiences to be obtained just beyond our borders. To the south in Bernardston the 3423-yard, nine-hole (soon to be 18) Crumpin-Fox Club is one of only two Robert Trent Jones designs in Massachusetts. Nearby at Williams College in Williamstown, sixty-five sand traps litter the 6185-yard, par 71 Taconic Golf Club. In western New Hampshire eighteen-hole courses are found at Keene (Bretwood Golf Course), Grantham (the challenging Eastman Golf Links), and nine-hole facilities in Lebanon (Farnham Hills) and Claremont (Claremont Country Club). The best bordering golf of all is found at Hanover Country Club, an eighteen-hole course (with four additional practice holes) owned by Dartmouth College. The Vale of Tempe, a one hundred-yard-wide gully which must be traversed several times, afflicts six of the eighteen holes, and tall pine trees intrude on the rest. On the opposite side of the state, a scant twenty-five miles from the border, Queensbury Country Club is an eighteen-hole New York State facility near Lake George with a $9.00 all-day rate. Look for it to open in late March, a few weeks before any Vermont clubs.

Crumpin-Fox Club	413-648-9101
Taconic Golf Club	413-458-9669
Bretwood Golf Course	603-352-0135
Claremont C.C.	603-542-9551
Farnham Hills C.C.	603-448-3323
Hanover C.C.	603-646-2000
Queensbury C.C.	518-793-3711

DRIVING RANGES

There are "stand alone" driving ranges at Rutland, Morrisville, Williston, South Burlington, St. Albans, West Brattleboro, and North New Haven. Furthermore, many of these courses in this book have a practice area, sometimes for members only, but many times open to anyone with their own shag bag. Last, you may actually buy a bucket of balls at the following courses: Basin Harbor, Crown Point, Lake Morey, Mt. Anthony, Mt. Snow, Quechee, Stowe, Stratton, Sugarbush, Woodstock.

Walter Barcomb: Alburg (with R.B. Ellison), Rocky Ridge (with E. Farrington), *Quarry Hill (par 3).

Ralph Martin Barton (1875–1941): Newport (original nine), *Wilmington, *Kingsbery Club.

Brad Caldwell: Kwiniaska.

Alexander Campbell: Basin Harbor (original nine).

Graham Cooke: Champlain (remodeled nine, added nine), Essex.

Geoffrey Cornish (1914-   ): Killington with Brian Silva, Basin Harbor (remodeled), Manchester, Stratton (Forest nine) with Brian Silva. With William G. Robinson (1941-   ), Mt. Snow, Quechee (36 holes), Stratton (Lake & Mountain nines), Farm Resort (par 3), Montague (remodeled), Ekwanok (remodeled eight holes).

Tom Devlin: Richford.

Francis Duane (1921-   ): Fox Run, Marble Island (remodeled).

Henry Duskett: Bomoseen.

Alex H. Findlay: *Old Pine.

William Flynn (1891-1945): *Hartwellville.

George Frazer: *Bristol.

Andrew Freeland: Waterbury Inn (now Blush Hill), *Barton.

Les Heon: Montpelier (remodeled), Northfield.

Michael Hurdzan (1943-   ): Barre (second nine), Newport (second nine).

Robert Trent Jones (1906-   ): Woodstock (current layout 1963), Sugarbush (with Francis Duane).

Marty Keene: West Bolton (with Xen Wheeler).

George Low, Sr.: Rutland (original nine).

William Mitchell (1912-1974): Crown Point, Stowe, Basin Harbor (remodeled nine, added nine), Brattleboro (remodeled), Equinox (remodeled).

Desmond Muirhead (1924-   ): Haystack.

Ralph Myhre: Middlebury.

Willie Park Jr. (1864-1925): St. Johnsbury.

Alex Reid: Orleans.

Horace Rollins: *Hyde Manor (with George Sargent).

Donald James Ross (1872-1948): Burlington, Woodstock (1930s).

George Salling: Lake Morey.

Brian Silva: Killington, Stratton (Forest nine) with Geoffrey Cornish.

Wayne Stiles (1884-1953): Brattleboro, Woodstock (added nine 1924). With John

*No longer exists

R. Van Kleek, Barre (original nine), Rutland (remodeled nine, added nine), *Brandon.

Herbert Bertram Strong (1879-1944): *Lake Shore.

Albert Tillinghast (1872-1942): Marble Island.

Walter Travis (1862-1927): Equinox, Woodstock (remodeled 1912), Ekwanok (with John Duncan Dunn [1874-1951]).

William Henry Tucker, Sr. (1871-1954): Woodstock (original nine: 1906).

Howard Watson (1907-   ): A.D. Dana Estate.

BIBLIOGRAPHY

Clarke, Fred C., Jr. *The Woodstock Country Club.* Privately published, 1959.

Colomb, Reggie. *Rutland Country Club: A Continuing Tradition.* Facts of publication unknown.

Cornish, Geoffrey, and Ronald E. Whitten. *The Golf Course.* New York: Rutledge Press, 1981.

Ekwanok Country Club. *Ekwanok Country Club 75th Anniversary.* Privately published, 1975.

English, John P. "Dorset's Claim As Oldest Club." *USGA Golf Journal* (September 1965): 16-19.

Fairbanks, Edward. *The Town of St. Johnsbury.* St. Johnsbury, Vt.: Cowles Press, 1914.

Hagarman, M. *More about Morristown 1935–1980.* 1981.

History of Mt. Anthony Country Club. Privately published, 1944.

Hyde Park, Vermont: Shire Town of Lamoille County. Essex Junction, Vt.: Essex Publishing Co., 1976.

James, Floyd. "Green Mountain Golf." *Vermont Life* 8, no. 4 (Summer 1954): 34–40.

Mahoney, Jack. *The Golf History of New England.* Wellesley, Ma.: Wellesley Press, 1973.

Martin, H.B. *Fifty Years of American Golf.* 2d ed. New York: Argosy-Antiquarian Ltd., 1966.

Merrill, Perry. *Montpelier: The Capital City's History, 1780–1976.* Montpelier, Vt.: Perry Merrill, 1976.

Miller, Richard. "Hole for One." *Town & Country* 140, no. 5079 (1986): 106–7.

Newman, Joseph. *Official Golf Guide of America 1899.* New York: Garden City Press, 1899.

Olman, John M., and Morton W. Olman. *Encyclopedia of Golf Collectibles.* Florence, Ala.: Books Americana, Inc., 1985.

Peper, George. *Golf Courses of the P.G.A. Tour.* New York: Harry N. Abrams, 1986.

Sargent, Porter E. *A Handbook on New England.* Boston: Sargent Press, 1916.

Shapiro, Mel. *A Turn of the Century Treasury.* Secaucus, N.J.: Castle Book Sales, Inc. 1986.

Slack, Ann, ed. *Mountain View Country Club 1898–1976.* 1976.

Vermont Development Agency. *Vermont Golf Directory*. Eds.: 1940, 1950, 1964, 1966. Montpelier, Vt.: Vermont Development Agency.

Vermont Peoples National Bank. "Brattleboro Country Club." *With Interest* (August 1926).

Wind, Herbert Warren. *The Story of American Golf*. New York: Farrar and Strauss, 1948.